A International Heroes Book

NELSON

MANDELA

Voice of Freedom

Libby Hughes

AN AUTHORS GUILD BACKINPRINT.COM EDITION

AN AUTHORS GUILD BACKINPRINT.COM EDITION

Published by iUniverse.com, Inc.

For information address:
iUniverse.com, Inc.
620 North 48th Street, Suite 201
Lincoln, NE 68504-3467
www.iuniverse.com

Originally published by Macmillan

Jacket: AP-Wide World Photos; AP-Wide World Photos-8, 11, 14, 25, 32, 35, 49,
59, 61, 68, 76, 78, 81, 83, 88, 100, 103, 114, 117, 121, 128; Author: 22, 41, 43, 116,
123, 131, 134; United Nations Photo Library: 12; Anglo American Corporation
of South Africa: 37

ISBN: 0-595-00733-3

Printed in the United States of America

Acknowledgments

Nelson Mandela, Tokyo Sexwale, Michael Owen, Jackie and Bill Stay, Patrick Evans and Mr. Jacobs of the South African Embassy, Judy Moon, Ian Wyllie, Major General Holomisa, Major Jones, the American Embassy in Pretoria, Minister of Justice Kobie Coetzee, Timothy Watson, Helen Joseph, and Robert Tucker.

Contents

To Mil, E. W., and J. F. S. for their loyalty
and support over the years.

Introduction

Getting into South Africa and getting to see Nelson Mandela in August of 1990 were major challenges. For five months, I had tried to obtain a visa from several South African consulates to visit South Africa to write this book on Nelson Mandela. After contacting the South Africans many times during each of those weeks, nothing was forthcoming. Finally, the day before I left for Johannesburg, the visa was granted and air expressed to the Atlanta airport.

Trying to secure an interview with Nelson Mandela was equally frustrating. During those same five months, prior to departing for South Africa, I contacted the ANC (African National Congress) and the State Department, plus many other sources, to schedule an interview. Only silence and stonewalling resulted.

Once I was in Johannesburg, I found 500 other journalists and writers, hoping for the same face-to-face encounter with Nelson Mandela. The prospects looked bleak. While touring in Soweto one day with some black friends, a series of coincidences led to a contact who arranged for me to meet with Mr. and Mrs. Mandela the next evening in their Soweto home. Behind high brick walls and an elaborate electronic system, my business manager and I entered the Mandela compound.

The tall, gentle-faced Nelson Mandela stood to greet us in his peach-and-lime colored living room. Friendly and soft-spoken, he introduced us to his two daughters, Zenani and Zindzi. Zenani, married to a Swazi prince and the mother of three children, was an undergraduate student at Boston University.

Then Winnie Mandela came in from a long day as a welfare and social worker for the ANC. Warm, attractive, strong, and articulate, she shared an affectionate embrace with her husband. That was a special moment. Obviously, Nelson Mandela adores his wife.

Once the Mandelas knew the purpose of my visit, I brought out my notebook and microcassette recorder. Mr. Mandela resisted this hurried attempt to interview him. "I don't want to answer you in a scrappy manner," he said. "Can you fly up to a game reserve where I will be vacationing? We can spend the day talking." That sounded fine. However, the very next day was the beginning of the tragic violence that erupted in Soweto over the next year. Although I was not able to see Mr. Mandela again, I had had the privilege of meeting him.

I had lived in South Africa for six years when apartheid was at its worst and when Nelson Mandela was defending himself during the treason trial. To come back 30 years later was a shock. The major cities were all but unrecognizable and the crumbling of apartheid was a welcome change. My telephone had been tapped for years. But the beauty of this country, especially in the Cape Province, had never changed.

My intent on this trip was to see all of Mandela's schools, universities, prisons, and friends. On one of these ventures, my friend and I drove through the Transkei, an independent homeland for four million blacks, to see Mandela's home villages. A Major General Holomisa gave us a car, driver, and interpreter. Bumping over miles of dirt roads, I saw the Mqekezweni village and the lime-washed hut where Nelson grew up with his cousins and uncle. We also saw Qunu, where Nelson and his sisters first romped over the hills under the watchful eyes of their mother.

Although denied permission to visit Robben Island, seven miles off the coast of Cape Town where Mandela spent 20 years in prison, my friend and I were allowed to stay near the harbor at Cowley House, where friends and relatives of political prisoners have free lodging and food before going by boat to Robben Island for a 30-minute visit.

To understand the history of apartheid is to understand Nelson Mandela and his struggle against its cruelty and injustices. As the world's most famous prisoner, Nelson Mandela turned his tragedy into triumph.

Libby Hughes
August 1991

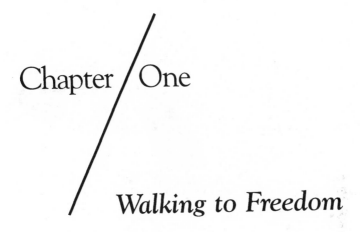

Chapter / One

Walking to Freedom

Nelson Mandela stepped into the sunlight of freedom on February 11, 1990. From a prison outside Cape Town, South Africa, he greeted a world that had waited over a quarter century for his release. Twenty-seven years earlier, the South African government had jailed him for his outspoken and militant resistance to apartheid, the system of racial segregation in South Africa.

Mandela walked proudly through the prison gates with his wife, Winnie, giving the African salute of the clenched fist. At 71 years of age, his hair was peppered with gray and his body was thin, but his walk still had a youthful spring to it. The first words Mandela spoke as a free man held no bitterness.

"I greet you all in the name of peace, democracy,

and freedom for all. I stand here before you not as a prophet but as a humble servant of you, the people. Your tireless and heroic sacrifices have made it possible for me to be here today. . . . I pay tribute to the mothers and wives and sisters of our nation. You are the rock-hard foundation of our struggle. Apartheid has inflicted more pain on you than anyone else," said Mandela to the group that was listening to his words.

As the Mandelas drove through the crowded streets of Cape Town, Mandela asked his chauffeur to stop. He stepped out, took a white baby into his arms, and posed for the young white couple eager to take his picture as if to symbolize that blacks and whites should live harmoniously in the future. Mandela's instincts as a politician had not been lost during those 27 years away from humanity.

Once his car had maneuvered through the masses of people, Mandela stood on the balcony of Cape Town's City Hall. The cheers from the crowd swelled into a chant, "Mandela," "Mandela," as he waved his arms and smiled. Nelson looked out across the crowded Grand Parade to the harbor, beyond where he had boarded a small wooden boat in 1962 and plowed through seven miles of choppy waters to Robben Island. There, on that isolated, drab island, he had spent over 25 years in musty cells, doing hard labor under the relentless sun. There, he had been separated

More than 57,000 Americans greeted Mandela when his motorcade traveled from Kennedy Airport to Brooklyn.

Addressing the United Nations General Assembly

from his wife and children. There, he had fought for the rights of prisoners and taught them the value of education.

Because of Mandela's global fame, he was immediately thrust into the political arena, in which he became the key spokesman for the African National Congress (ANC). This was an organization formed in 1912 by black Africans to protect their rights and to protest the unjust treatment under apartheid. Within months of his release, Mandela began to travel worldwide to speak out against apartheid.

In the United States, Mandela's ten-day tour in June 1990 brought praise and respect for the dignified way that he had survived almost 30 years in prison for resisting racial injustices. He was received as a hero and an inspiration to African Americans.

After addressing the United Nations General Assembly, Mandela, who was not an elected official of any government, was invited to address a joint session of the United States Congress, only the third private individual ever asked to do so.

"Let us join hands with all people of conscience throughout the world. . . . Let justice triumph without delay. Blessed are the peacemakers," were the closing words from Nelson Mandela to Americans. The audience of senators, congressmen, and guests gave him a standing ovation when he finished.

Since his college days, Mandela's qualities of leadership, honesty, and moderation had been recognized by fellow law students of all races. With an active law practice and a gift for speech making, Mandela had become a respected figure within and without the ranks of the ANC.

From the time he was a young boy, Mandela had heard the tribal elders discussing the injustices inflicted upon blacks by whites. The elders told him of wars between these two races and of territory seized from black chieftains by whites. Only when Mandela

Mandela acknowledges applause before a joint meeting of Congress in June 1990.

moved out of the black territories—also called reserves, Bantustans, or homelands—into white populated areas did he experience treatment that was based on the color of his skin. In these white areas, he would learn that he could not go where whites could go because of apartheid, and he could live only where the whites told him he could live—far from good land and good jobs. He also found out that the best jobs were reserved for whites.

The word *apartheid* means apartness. Almost from the arrival of the white man in the seaport of Cape Town, South Africa, in 1652, the whites have separated themselves from nonwhites. By 1948 apartheid had become an official policy for maintaining white supremacy and depriving blacks of their rights to freedom and power. Apartheid even extended segregation to so-called Cape Coloreds (a mixture of white and black races), Indians, and Asians.

The Coloreds were a tragic group. They belonged neither to the blacks nor the whites, but the rules of apartheid still applied to them.

For whites, apartheid was a comfortable system. They had a high standard of living in which black servants cleaned their homes, cooked their meals, and worked in their gardens. But apartheid separated black husbands from their wives and children. Husbands and sons had to leave their families behind in isolated homelands, hundreds of miles away, to find work in the cities.

There were ten of these black homelands scattered throughout South Africa. They were first established by the Land Acts of 1913 and 1936 in which 13 percent of the worst land in the country was given to blacks. Gouged by erosion and full of rocks, much of the land could not be cultivated. Since blacks outnumbered whites by five to one, the white government hoped to keep the majority of blacks in the homelands. As a young man, Mandela was a victim of these land laws.

To control the number of blacks coming into urban areas to find work, black males were forced to carry identity cards, called pass laws, which were instituted by the white government in 1936. The passes were required for finding jobs, for traveling anywhere in the country, and for being out after a curfew hour for blacks. Without the proper papers, a black male could be arrested and jailed. The pass laws were greatly hated by blacks. During his years as a lawyer, Mandela defended his black clients accused under these unfair rules.

When blacks came to the cities and found work, they could not live near the white suburbs, but were forced to live in townships set aside for blacks in the wastelands outside the cities. Here, blacks had to live in squalid conditions without plumbing and electricity. Thousands of people were crowded together in thousands of tin or wooden shacks. For those families not living in the homelands, the police could raid their homes any time of day or night and take black men and women to jail, leaving crying children unattended.

Against this background of inhumane and unequal treatment of blacks, Nelson Mandela dedicated his life to his people in overturning this barbaric system. There would be many personal sacrifices for this devotion. And yet, he loved his country and hoped that all races could live in harmony within a democratic, constitutional system.

South Africa is one of the most beautiful countries in the world. It has four large provinces. There is the Cape Province with the Kimberley Diamond Mines and the rich vineyards on the flanks of Table Mountain, overlooking Cape Town's harbor. There is the Orange Free State, which holds the tawny desert of the Karoo. In the Transvaal Province, there are rich deposits of gold. Natal Province has forest-green hills and valleys, a coastline of beaches, and acres of sugarcane fields.

Against a backdrop of such beauty, the inequities of apartheid seemed even more tragic to Nelson Mandela.

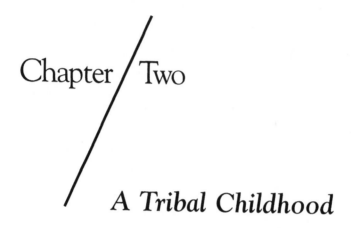

Chapter / Two

A Tribal Childhood

In the eastern belly of South Africa, the billowy clouds hang low and almost touch the treeless hills. This is the Transkei, a black homeland that stretches inland from the Indian Ocean. Since 1976 the Transkei has been an independent black state. Sometimes in winter, the clouds look like a ceiling of corrugated iron, casting long shadows across the village huts.

Here, Nelson Mandela's life had its beginnings in a tribal village. Deep in the heartland of the Transkei, he was born on July 18, 1918, the son of Hendry Mphakanyiswa Gadla (Henry Mandela). Henry was a chieftain from the Thembu tribe, related to the larger Xhosa tribe. Nelson's mother, Nosekeni Fanny, was Henry's third wife.

Nelson was born in Mvezo, along the Umbashe

River, which flows eastward into the Indian Ocean. While he was still a baby, his parents moved to the small village of Qunu, located on the slopes outside Umtata, the capital of the Transkei.

From the age of five, Nelson shepherded his family's cattle and goats up and down the tawny slopes of Qunu. Happily, he played around his mother's kraal, her own little "village." The kraal consisted of three *rondavels*, or round huts, with thatched roofs. The chief of the entire family compound had four or more wives. Usually each wife had a kraal of three huts and a plot of ground for raising corn. Each hut had a different purpose: one was used for sleeping; one was used for storing food; and one was used for eating in. Generally, the outside walls of the huts were whitewashed.

Inside the kitchen hut, Nelson's mother cooked on a grate over the hole in the center of the mud floor. Under the grate were corncobs used for firewood. The smoke from the iron pot of mealie (corn) porridge would spiral upward to escape through the two windows on opposite walls of the hut. When the meal was ready, Mandela, his two older sisters, his baby sister Leabie, and his mother would sit cross-legged on the ground, eating from their enamel bowls. Often, a baby lamb, goat, or guinea fowl would wander into the hut and nibble the scraps.

Mandela's mother could not read or write, but she

had become a devout Methodist and sent him and his sisters to the mission school in Qunu. It was at this school that Mandela received his English name. At birth, his parents had given him the tribal name of Rohihiahla, meaning "stirring up trouble." Yet, as a young boy, he seemed quiet and cooperative. Apparently, one of the white schoolteachers could not pronounce his name, and one day she finally said, "From now on, your name is Nelson." And so, the name Nelson stayed with him.

Nelson's father, Chief Henry Mandela, had been a brave and outspoken leader. During World War I, he had fought with the South African army against the Germans in South-West Africa. Later, he was appointed to a committee for whites and blacks to discuss problems in the Transkei. However, Henry did not like to take orders from other tribal leaders. Although Henry was only one of several chiefs, he dared to challenge the main chief. As a result, he lost his title of chief and his wealth, which meant he could barely support his four wives and twelve children.

Nelson, his mother, and sisters suffered greatly from their father's loss of power and money. Nelson had to wear his father's old clothes to the church school. The other children often made fun of the ex-chief's son, now poorer than they, but Nelson ignored their taunts.

Since Nelson was the only boy among his three sisters, he had a special relationship with his father. Often, Henry would tell Nelson stories about their ancestors and show him where Henry's great-grandfather was on the family tree. Henry hoped that Nelson would become king of the Thembu tribe some day.

The death of his father from an illness changed Mandela's life. Just before Henry died, he asked his nephew, paramount chief of all the Thembus, Jongintaba Dalindyebo, to educate the 10-year-old boy. In the tribal custom, Chief Jongintaba took on the responsibility for Nelson's future.

Nelson recalled those childhood memories in a letter he wrote from prison in 1977. "Mother could neither read nor write and had no means to send me to school. Yet, a member of our clan educated me from the elementary school right up to Fort Hare and never expected any refund. According to our custom, I was his child and his responsibility. . . . " Mandela favored many parts of the tribal system.

Shortly after his father's death, Nelson left his mother and three sisters to go and live with his new guardian. In 1928 Chief Jongintaba arrived in his Ford V-8 to take Nelson and his tin trunk of clothes to the village of Mqekezweni, which was about 20 miles away over rough roads and hills. There, Nelson was in-

The hut in Mqekezweni where Mandela grew up.

troduced to Nkosikasi No-England (perhaps a nick-
name against Great Britain), the chief's wife, who wel-
comed him as if he were her own son. She brought him
to the lime-washed hut that he would share with her
son, Justice. Over the years these two boys would become closer than brothers. In the hut, there were two
beds and a table with an oil lamp beside which the
boys could do their homework. Outside his window,
Nelson saw the distant hills of Qunu across the valley
and thought of his mother and sisters.

Nelson started attending the small Methodist

school in the village compound a few hundred yards away. He studied in a small classroom, which was shared with older children. He learned English and geography, along with history and the Xhosa language. The missionary school education was considered much better than that of the government schools. Nelson also went willingly and happily to Sunday school at the Methodist church, next door to the little school.

Education did not occupy all of 12-year-old Nelson's time—there were chores for him to do, too. He herded the cattle and milked the cows at sundown. With Justice and others he hunted birds with a homemade slingshot. Once the birds were caught, the boys cleaned and cooked them over the kitchen grate at his aunt's large home next to his hut. When he wasn't in school or doing chores, Nelson liked to wade and splash in the narrow river at the bottom of the hill and play with the round black stones from the riverbed. From the riverbanks, he threw them far or skipped them across the top of the water. Later, in prison, Mandela remembered those happy days.

The town of Mqekezweni was larger than Qunu, and though the countryside was hilly like Qunu, it was muddier and full of rocks. The rains would rush down the barren hillsides, gouging deep ravines into the slope and leaving jagged ruts in the village compound.

In the village center there was a rectangular courthouse where the legal business for Nelson's tribe, the Thembu, was conducted. Across from this courthouse was the royal dining hall. Here, elder members from other districts gathered for their evening meals and then spent many hours talking. Nelson and other favored youngsters were allowed to listen to the tales of history spun by these old men. Nelson sat on the floor in wide-eyed silence.

One of the wisest chiefs to talk at the royal dining hall was Zwelibhagile Joyi, who greatly influenced Nelson. From this wrinkled and bent old man, Nelson learned how the Thembus dated back to the 15th century. The old man further told Nelson how the white people had deliberately encouraged controversies among the Pondo, Thembu, Zulu, and Xhosa tribes in order to take away their lands from them. This probably was the beginning of black against black violence, which would resurface again in 1990 and 1991.

During the 1800s, the whites took advantage of these tribal disputes and bought land from the chiefs or seized it through force. There were nine Kaffir (an insulting term for a black African) Wars waged against the whites from 1779 to 1836. Most of these wars were fought in the area between the Great Fish River in the Ciskei, a black homeland, and the Kei River in the Transkei.

Violence in Tokoza claimed 700 lives in one month in 1990.

The fighting between the Xhosas and Zulus in Natal and Transvaal provinces in the 1990s reflected those same deep tribal and political divisions that existed more than two centuries ago. Even today, the white population has been blamed for encouraging this black-against-black violence in an effort to show that the blacks are not ready to assume majority power in South Africa.

In 1910 South Africa had called itself the "Union

of South Africa," a part of the British Commonwealth. Many Britons arrived in South Africa in the
1800s. The two main white nationalities were the
Afrikaners and the British. The Afrikaners were the
descendants of early Dutch, French, and German set-
tlers who had intermarried. The Afrikaans language
resulted from the combination of the three languages.
There are still two languages in South Africa—
Afrikaans and English.

From 1830 onward, the British tried to abolish
slavery in the Cape Province, but the white
Afrikaners resisted. They needed slaves to work on
their farms. Finally, the Afrikaner Boers (farmers) left
the Cape in 1836 to push northward in their ox wag-
ons to find land to farm. This event was known as the
Great Trek. In 1880 and 1886, the Afrikaners had discovered gold and diamonds. The British headed
north, too, to attack the Afrikaners. This was the beginning of the famous Boer War (from 1899 to 1902).
The British won, but bitter feelings still remain from
that war.

At school, Nelson was fascinated by South Africa's history. Unfortunately, school in Mqekezweni
only went as far as the seventh grade, and Chief Jongintaba knew he had to honor his promise to oversee
Nelson's education.

After a final year in the neighboring village of

Qokolweni, Nelson traveled to Engcobo in the western Transkei to attend high school in Clarkebury.

During vacations, Nelson spent more and more time in the tribal courthouse, observing the legal process of cross-examining witnesses, presenting evidence, defending clients, and making judgments.

When Nelson was 19, his uncle planned to send him to the university. To prepare for this, Nelson was sent south to a Methodist school, called Healdtown, in the Ciskei, near the University of Fort Hare. He graduated from Healdtown in 1938.

In 1939 Nelson was admitted to the University of Fort Hare in the Ciskei, near the border of the Cape Province. Proud of his ward, Chief Jongintaba outfitted him in a brand-new, three-piece suit. Nelson could hardly wait for his first term to begin.

Chapter / Three

Leaving Home

Eager to begin his journey to the University of Fort Hare, Nelson was driven to the town of Alice in the Ciskei.

Around every twist and turn of the mountain passes through the Transkei, Nelson saw incredible beauty. Against the tawny mesas and torpedo-shaped hills were huts washed in colors of pink, purple, turquoise, yellow, or white. They were dotted in terraces up and down each mountainside.

As the travelers wound up and down the narrow roads, cattle lumbered to the side or in front of them while goats and sheep darted unpredictably at the passing cars, which had to constantly beep their horns.

Closer to the coast were tree farms on the green

folds of the hillsides. On the banks of the jade green river waters there were women washing clothes and hanging them to dry on bushes.

Driving down the final mountain pass out of the Transkei, they came to the bridge over the Great Fish River, deep below in the rocky canyon.

Three hours from his home village, Nelson reached the town of Alice, which was southwest over gentle rolling hills of dry desert and fanned to the Hogsback Mountain range in the distance. The country area around the town of Alice was flatter and greener than Nelson's home village. People who approached the college campus could see a tunnel of trees along the main road before turning into the small cluster of buildings at Fort Hare.

The school had been established in 1916 by a group of Christian missionaries who originated the idea of providing a place of higher learning for bright young black students who come from all parts of the African continent. Over the years, Fort Hare gained the reputation of being a training ground for future African leaders.

When Nelson arrived in 1939, he joined the 180-person student body (5,000 today), of which 12 were women. His dormitory was Wesley Hall, built by Methodists, who named it after their founder, John Wesley.

The different church denominations, such as Anglican, Presbyterian, and Methodist, built their own dormitories, or hostels as they were called, for sons of that particular congregation. This saved the university from any additional expenses. The hostels were usually built in a rectangular style, of white cement or stucco with small, barren rooms—just large enough for a bed and desk. They were located some distance away from Stewart Hall, the main classroom building, and from the dining hall in the Christian Union Building with its round porthole windows and a terra-cotta roof.

The library, Stewart Hall, and the gymnasium were all grouped together in a small quadrangle, making it easy for the students to move around. Stewart Hall, where Nelson attended most of his classes, was—and still is—a severe, long, narrow, two-story white structure. It was the heart of the university during Nelson's years.

Today, the Fort Hare campus is crowded with modern, brightly colored offices and lecture halls. A rash of yellow and orange flowers fan across the landscape of brick sidewalks and towering trees. A new octagon-shaped art gallery holds a collection of works by the best black artists in southern Africa.

In a studious atmosphere from 1939–1941, the tall, athletic Mandela became popular, making friends easily. His professors liked him, too. Although he was a serious and thoughtful student, his booming laughter often echoed through the corridors of Stewart Hall. This irrepressible joy, coupled with an intense quest for knowledge, became Mandela's trademark throughout the years. His interest in black history deepened, and he spent many hours in the libraries researching the records to confirm the stories he had heard from the tribal elders. Because of this research, he came to resent white writers of history textbooks for not recording the black history that Chief Joyi and the library records had described.

The American boxer Joe Louis had been one of Nelson's boyhood heroes and not long after Mandela's arrival at Fort Hare, he took up amateur boxing in the gymnasium. His broad and tall frame made him a fearsome looking opponent, and the rigorous athletic training taught him the value of exercise that later helped him through many years of prison life.

Nelson found time for a social life, too. He and a few of his friends had been learning how to dance—the fox-trot and waltz. Anxious to test their accomplishments by dancing with some girls, they sneaked away from the campus one Saturday night and went to a respectable dance hall not far away. In his three-piece suit, Nelson felt like the handsome young man he was. Carefully, he looked at all the girls and, spot-

Mandela and Oliver Tambo enjoy a reunion – the first time they had met in more than 28 years.

ting a very pretty one, invited her to dance. As they glided gracefully around the dance floor, he asked her name. When he discovered she was the wife of one of his professors, he was embarrassed and returned her to her husband. Fortunately, the professor did not report him for being away from campus and at a place that was off-limits to students. Nelson always noticed pretty girls and enjoyed wearing finely tailored clothes.

During the first two years at Fort Hare, Nelson made some lasting friendships. He met Oliver Tambo, who would become his law partner and president of the African National Congress. Tambo's upbringing was similar to Nelson's. He had grown up in Pondoland in the Transkei, and also had a religious background.

Tambo and Mandela were compatible in their political thinking about justice and democracy for blacks. However, Nelson reacted more quickly to political and social issues, stating them openly and publicly without fear of consequences—much like his own father.

In fact, an incident at Fort Hare toward the end of his sophomore year cut short his university career. Some of the students were protesting against the quality of school food. Nelson joined them in their protest and also in their demand that the university authorities give more power to the Students' Representative Council. The authorities refused. Even after Nelson was threatened with suspension, he refused to stop pressing his demands. He was sent home. Although he was unhappy about leaving his studies, Mandela felt more strongly about standing by his principles.

He reluctantly returned to Mqekezweni and faced Chief Jongintaba. The chief demanded that Nelson apologize to the Fort Hare president and resume his education. But Nelson stood firm.

Irritated by Nelson's stubbornness, Chief Jongintaba decided that it was time for Nelson to get married. He secretly arranged for *lobola*. (Lobola is a gift or payment of cattle to the family of the bride.) Chief

Jongintaba agreed to pay lobola for a plump young woman from a good family. When Nelson heard of this plan, he rebelled and, joined by his cousin, Justice, he planned to run away. The two penniless cousins had to think of a way to get cash quickly, so they sold two of the chief's fine oxen. Before the chief could find out, the boys packed their things and headed toward the big city of Johannesburg by bus and train.

Johannesburg was a magic word to young black men. Called the "city of gold" because of its gold mines, "Jo-burg" symbolized for them the way to escape farm life and small villages for the excitement of city life.

Nelson and Justice stepped off the train in Johannesburg in 1941. The city was big. Buildings stretched endlessly into the sky. The Transkei and the town of Alice seemed like sleepy places compared to the throbbing activity of this city of a million people. As Nelson and Justice wandered down the main streets, well-dressed people were walking at a rapid pace. Black citizens were expected to step aside for whites.

At night, the blinking neon signs and the cluster of buildings outlined against the dark sky were very exciting for two young men from a small village.

Finding a relative's home was the first priority. Miles outside the towering city of Johannesburg were the native townships and slums for black Africans. On

Johannesburg from the air. The gold mines are in the background.

their way to Alexandra, one of the four native townships, the two cousins saw some beautiful houses be-
longing to wealthy white people in the suburbs around
Jo-burg. In contrast, Nelson was shocked at the poor
shacks, dusty roadways, and strong smell from the sewers in the townships. The shacks were without electricity, running water, or indoor plumbing, and they
were miles away from the workplaces.

Transportation took time and was costly for the

inhabitants. Many blacks had left their families and homelands to find better jobs and earn more money to send back home. Young men were separated from their families, friends, and tribal customs. This separation and the depressing living conditions often led them to crime and drinking.

Each morning, Nelson could smell the mealie porridge cooking and see the smoke coming from each shack, causing a heavy smog over the township. Men were leaving their shanties early to catch the buses to their jobs, which could be from 10 to 20 miles away, while women looked after the children or went to the white suburbs to clean houses and cook meals for their white "master" and "missus."

The two young men planned to go to the Crown Mines in search of work. A relative of theirs was employed there and spoke to the authorities about hiring them. The mines were run by whites, but the miners were all black, and black labor was in demand. Johannesburg, in the full light of day, kept its enchantment. But this time, they saw the mountains or mesas of gold dumps, the leftover material from the refined gold, scattered around the city. When the wind blew, it swept the gold dust across roads, offices, townships, and homes, leaving a carpet of sand everywhere. (Later, trees and wild grasses would be planted in the mine dumps to hold the sand down.)

The Gold Mine Museum, Johannesburg. Here a mine worker, using a jackhammer, shows the modern way gold is drilled.

When Nelson and Justice arrived at the Crown Mines, they were hired. Nelson accepted a temporary job as a security guard, in hopes of becoming one of the few black clerks in the office. Justice was willing to become a miner.

In the brief time they were working at the mine, Nelson observed what the lives of the black miners were like. Every day an elevator took the miners two miles under the earth's surface. In the damp tunnels, they drilled the rock walls in search of gold treasure. The loosened rock ore was brought aboveground and processed for the gold.

In the 1940s, each young black signed a year's contract. Their starting wages were 25 or 30 cents a day, which they sent home to their families. The men lived in barracks and slept on bunks of concrete slabs. Only Sundays were free days within the compound, and colorful tribal dances were usually performed for tourists. With at least 50 different tribes represented in the miners' ranks, the costumed dancers entertained many foreign visitors and kept the single men occupied and out of trouble.

However, Nelson and Justice did not get to serve out their contracts. Within a few days of their arrival at the mines, Chief Jongintaba, a powerful and respected chief even among whites, had traced the boys there and demanded that they return to the village. Both Nelson and Justice were fired immediately. Justice decided to go home, but Nelson was determined to stay in Johannesburg. He persuaded the chief to let him finish his undergraduate degree by correspondence. The chief agreed to help him pay the tuition fees, but Nelson would have to pay his own room and board.

Chapter / Four

Love, Law, and Politics

To come from a simple tribal hut and go to a big city was a big jump for young Africans who had never been away from home. However, the young men who flocked to the cities wanted the excitement of a job where things were happening. Some of these young men were lonely and fell into bad company, but Nelson Mandela was not one of them. He had been parted from his mother and sisters since he was ten years old, and he had been away at boarding school and the university. All of this had prepared him for the adventures ahead.

Nelson had to find a room in one of the townships outside Johannesburg. He soon rented a room from Mr. and Mrs. Schreiner Baduza in Alexandra township. With his small savings, he had to pay rent, bus fare, and food, so not much, if anything, was left over. Sometimes, he had to ask his landlords to allow him an extension on payment, until he found a steady job. They often invited him to join them on Sundays for their main meal. This helped to satisfy his youthful appetite, and it cut down on at least one expense.

Many years later, while in prison, Mandela thought back on these early days, appreciating the people who had done him so many kindnesses during those difficult times as a young man.

After a few months, he moved to the next street at the invitation of Reverend and Mrs. Mabuto to live in their small home. They treated Nelson like a son and offered advice and comments on some of the things he did. For example, Mrs. Mabuto disapproved of his dating young women who were not part of the Xhosa tribe. The older generations living in the cities still clung to the values and traditions of the tribe. Each tribe had its own language and culture that had endured through centuries. Therefore, tribal loyalties were very deep and lasting. But Nelson did not feel bound by tribal ties. Though he cherished his roots and history as part of his heritage, his ideas were more progressive.

Despite the poverty, squalor, and stench of the townships, Nelson developed a special feeling of attachment for Johannesburg and its townships. He

A township on the outskirts of Cape Town

liked hearing the cries of children playing in the dusty alleys. The smoke-filled dawns made him feel hopeful for what each day would bring. He liked to see the outline of jagged rooftops silhouetted against the orange sky at sundown.

When the darkness of an African night settled on the townships, the young men went to the *shebeens*, which were nightclubs in private homes. There they heard African music, danced with young ladies, or

talked and laughed with one another. The shrill sound
of the wooden flute called a penny whistle could be
heard in every corner of the township.

As he searched for a job in 1941, Nelson gained
a secret admirer. She was a young nurse named Evelyn
Ntoko Mase. Evelyn had seen the tall, handsome
Mandela and learned of his need for some kind of em-
ployment. She told her best friend, Albertina, at the
Johannesburg General Hospital about this man from
the Transkei. Evelyn also wanted Nelson to meet her
cousin, Walter Sisulu, a businessman in Johannesburg. Besides, Walter was engaged to Albertina!

When Walter Sisulu and Nelson met, they immediately established a friendship that would last
through the many years ahead. Although only a few
years older than Nelson, Walter became a mentor-
father figure to him. Sisulu ran his own small real es-
tate agency, which rented and sold what little land
was available to blacks. He offered Nelson the opportunity to become a salesman at two pounds (five dol-
lars) a month, with a commission on whatever he sold.
Nelson accepted.

Eventually, Walter asked Nelson if he would like
to move to the Johannesburg township in Orlando
West, where Walter's mother took in washing for
white women. Again, Nelson accepted.

Under Walter's encouragement, Nelson finished

Mandela's longtime friend, Walter Sisulu

his college degree through correspondence school in 1942. Walter bought him a suit for his graduation from the University of South Africa. It was a proud moment for both men.

After graduation, Nelson decided to study law. The days at the feet of his tribal elders as well as his student protests at Fort Hare had made a lasting impression on Nelson. Walter offered to help him through law school at Witwatersrand University in

Johannesburg, high on the ridge overlooking the city. This was a university for whites, but qualified blacks were allowed to enter until 1956, when blacks were barred from all white universities. In 1942 when Nelson began studying at the Faculty of Law, Walter found him a job as a clerk in the white law office of Witkin, Sidelsky, and Eidelman.

In the meantime, Nelson had begun a relationship with Evelyn, who was finishing her nurse's training. Since Evelyn was Walter's cousin, she was often in and out of the Sisulu house. The romance between them grew.

By 1944 Evelyn and Nelson were married, and they moved in with Evelyn's sister where they didn't have to pay rent. Both of them were working, Nelson part-time and Evelyn as a full-time nurse, leaving very little time for the couple to be together.

The new husband found himself more and more involved in politics. The discrimination against blacks in South Africa had been more apparent to Nelson since living in Johannesburg. Everywhere he went there were signs for "Europeans" (whites) and "Non-Europeans" (blacks). He was a second-class citizen because of the color of his skin.

Nelson felt that his training as a lawyer could prepare him for helping his people and making changes in the law. His contacts and intellectual discussions with Indians, Coloreds, and liberal-thinking whites reinforced this decision.

Nelson was breaking other racial barriers by befriending Indians like Ismail Meer, J. H. Singh, Ahmed Kathrada, and Dr. Nadoo—names that would be associated with him throughout the years. Traditionally, the Africans and Indians were unfriendly to one another. The Indians felt they were more deserving of rights and privileges than the blacks, creating bad feelings between the two groups.

Harry Schwartz, a white South African lawyer who went to law school with Nelson Mandela and who was appointed as South Africa's ambassador to the United States in 1991, remembered those student days. "We were going to lectures early in the morning and late in the afternoon, so we could work and earn a living during the day. We both took part in student politics. Nelson was concerned with the black liberation struggle. He was a very dedicated, intense person."

As Nelson's political interest grew, Walter Sisulu influenced Nelson and his friend Oliver Tambo, who moved back to Johannesburg, to attend some meetings of the ANC with him. Enthusiastic about its philosophy and will to fight for basic human rights, they joined in 1944.

Once they were part of the ANC, they realized it

had become more of a discussion group over the years and less concerned with action. Although the ANC had intended to make the white government give them the vote and allow them to be represented in the parliamentary system, nothing had happened. The ANC had become a voice for millions of black Africans, but nothing more.

Therefore, Nelson, Oliver Tambo, and others started a Youth League in 1944 as part of the ANC. Like most young men, Nelson hoped to use the Youth League to change things. Nelson was on its executive committee. When he became general secretary of the League, he brought a feeling of stability and harmony to the group. His air of assurance, leadership, and knowledge of the law inspired his followers.

The bright young men of the Youth League hoped to energize the members of the ANC and so reach a broader part of the black population. They published this statement of their aims: "The Congress Youth League must be the brains-trust and power-station of the spirit of African nationalism; the spirit of African self-determination; the spirit that is so discernible in the thinking of our youth. It must be an organization where young African men and women will meet and exchange ideas in an atmosphere pervaded by a common hatred of oppression."

In 1945 the Mandelas had become proud parents

of a baby boy whom they called Thembi. Another boy, Makgatho, was born in 1950, and a girl, Makaziwe, in 1954. Nelson also assumed other family responsibilities in 1945. His mother came from Qunu to live with them, as did his youngest sister, Leabie. He would guide Leabie through her high school education. Like his uncle, Nelson accepted the customary obligation to care for his relatives. In return, as Evelyn's and Nelson's schedules grew more hectic, Leabie and Nosekeni were helpful as baby-sitters.

By the time World War II was over, young Nelson had developed a network of friends who joined him in the struggle against apartheid. Some were former students and professors from Fort Hare, others were Indians at the University of Witwatersrand, while still others included a small group of whites.

Among these new friends, Mandela met a few Socialists and Communists in the white community who supported the ANC and all nonwhites in their cause for justice. Joe Slovo, a Marxist and fellow law student, would become an influential, lifelong friend. Nelson learned about Communist ideas from reading the books by Karl Marx (the German philosopher and economist who developed the Communist system of socialism) and Vladimir Lenin (the Russian who studied Marx and led the Communist revolution in Russia).

Because of his Christian upbringing, Nelson did not feel comfortable with all the ideas of communism, some of which were against all religion. On the other hand, communism had similarities to the tribal system; in both systems people were expected to live in communal groups and help one another. Therefore, Nelson read the ideas set forth by Marx and Lenin with interest. In later years, Nelson would find himself under attack by the government, named as a Communist.

After law classes and on weekends, these young men talked long and late, mostly about current South African politics. They were also influenced by the fact that all over Africa, after World War II, national movements were beginning to form to gain independence from colonial rule: Movements sprang up in Kenya, Nigeria, Ghana, and Rhodesia among other territories.

From 1948 onward, the British influence in South Africa lessened. Because the British Commonwealth did not approve of South Africa's racial policies, the Afrikaners were more determined than ever to strive for independence from Britain.

There were two main political parties in South Africa—the Nationalist Party and the United Party. Both had only white members. The National Party was made up of conservative Afrikaners who support-

A 1952 photo of Mandela taken in his law office in Johannesburg.

ed apartheid. The United Party, under the leadership of Jan Christian Smuts, was slightly more moderate. Smuts, a friend of Winston Churchill, became an international statesman during World War II and helped structure the United Nations organization. Despite Smuts's international reputation, the South African elections in 1948 brought the Nationalist Party to power, and strengthened the grip of apartheid on the blacks of South Africa.

For blacks, the ANC, led by preacher and teacher Albert Luthuli from 1952 to 1967, became a refuge for all their rage and aspirations, oppressed even further by the election of the Nationalists in 1948.

Mandela referred to the agonies of blacks in a speech he made in the 1960s. "Since 1912 and year after year thereafter . . . the African people have discussed the shameful misdeeds of those who rule the country . . . in condemnation of the grinding poverty, the low wages, the acute shortage of land, the inhumane exploitation and the whole policy of white domination. But instead of more freedom, repression began to grow in volume and intensity."

Through the ANC and a small core of white liberals, Nelson and his group of lawyers and politically active friends hoped to change the oppressive life of blacks to one that would be more free and just.

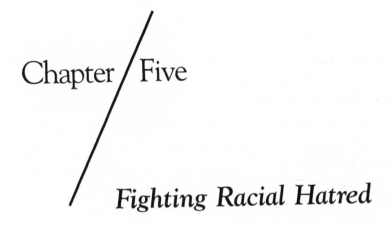

Chapter / Five

Fighting Racial Hatred

Throughout the late 1940s and early 1950s, Mandela was up early every morning in his Johannesburg home, usually before daylight. No matter how long he had to study or how late his political meetings kept him, he jogged around the dusty alleys and unpaved streets of the township by himself or with one of his small sons. Afterward, he returned to prepare breakfast.

With the increasing pressures on Evelyn and Nelson, time with their two boys was limited. They shared parental responsibilities. Nelson enjoyed shopping for groceries and bathing the children or talking to them about many subjects. However, as his political activities and travels increased, he was able to see his family less and less.

His second son, Makgatho, recalled those early years: "He bought us ice cream. We loved his stories. He took us to meetings and explained words to us. He was athletic. We jogged together. He never beat us. His lessons were worse than a beating. Once I lied to him about money I needed to go swimming. When he found out, he could not understand how I could do such a thing." And yet, Nelson himself had stolen corncobs as a youngster and two oxen from his chief.

Although much of Nelson's time was devoted to work and studying law, his involvement in politics became deeper in the 1940s and 1950s. Most of the laws of apartheid were passed during this period. The man responsible for many of them was Dr. Hendrik F. Verwoerd, minister of Native Affairs from 1948 until his election as prime minister in 1958. To combat world criticism of South Africa's racial policies, Verwoerd became the architect of more homelands, pretending to give blacks more independence in their own areas. In fact, however, Verwoerd and the Nationalists created a catalog of laws to oppress nonwhites.

Beginning in 1949, the Mixed Marriages Act prevented anyone from marrying outside his or her own race. If two people from different races fell in love, they would be forbidden to marry and raise a family.

The Population Registration Act of 1950 required every person to register and identify his or her race. All nonwhites found this distasteful. Their declaration as a member of a specific race determined how they would be treated.

Also in 1950, the Group Areas Act determined where blacks or any nonwhites could live. This divided the races even further and lumped blacks together in tribal homelands or urban townships. In 1953, for example, 58,000 Africans were moved out of the Sophiatown township because the whites of Johannesburg wanted to take the land for themselves! The same law prevented educated and middle-class Coloreds and Indians from moving out of slum areas into better neighborhoods.

Probably the act with the broadest powers was the Suppression of Communism Act, also passed in 1950 after the Communist party was banned for good. Anyone could be arrested for any reason and banned or confined to house arrest from 90 days to six months. For a banning or an arrest, no proof was needed and no appeal could be made. Once the banning period expired, the ban could be renewed again and again. If any black looked as if he might be an organizer or a leader, he would be arrested under the Suppression of Communism Act. Supposedly there were 2,000 known Communists in South Africa, which included whites as well as nonwhites.

The mood of the world had become anti-Communist in the 1950s. In the United States, the obsession against communism was publicized during the Senate hearings in Washington, D.C., led by Republican Senator Joseph P. McCarthy. Many Americans, particularly in the arts, were accused of being Communists and some were sent to jail or blacklisted from work. The epidemic of anticommunism spread to South Africa and gave the white government an excuse for arresting anyone who defied these laws.

In 1951 the Bantu Authorities Act was signed into law. It was an attempt to retribalize the black Africans. The word *Bantu* means "native," and by keeping black Africans in a tribal state, mentally and geographically, the whites could control them.

Finally, the Bantu Education Act in 1953 made Africans attend their own schools and be taught in their own native languages through the primary grades. The white government was afraid that learning English would draw the blacks into the mainstream of the world. Therefore, in 1957 the government removed blacks from government schools, from 4,000 missionary schools, and from access to any colleges of mixed races. This was the best way to keep blacks oppressed. The money spent for the education of whites was five and a half times greater than that for blacks. Nelson called education "the greatest weapon for the future" and knew that the Bantu Education Act was a backward step.

At a 1953 ANC conference in the Transvaal, Mandela told his people: "You must defend the right of African parents to decide the kind of education that shall be given to their children. . . . If it becomes dangerous and impossible to have alternative schools, then you must make every home, every shack, every rickety structure a center for learning for our children."

Church leaders and moderate thinkers came to the rescue of black education by finding 1,000 volunteer teachers and forming the African Education Movement, under the guidance of Father Trevor Huddleston, a white Anglican priest in Johannesburg.

As the walls of racial division were growing higher, so was racial hatred under Verwoerd's legislations. Another despised law, established in 1953, was the Reservation of Separate Amenities Act, which prevented nonwhites from using buses, trains, theaters, restaurants, hotels, and hospitals reserved for whites. Separate facilities for blacks were inferior.

Mandela and members of the Youth League attempted to fight each new law by demanding more action and less talk from the ANC. They challenged the old guard at an ANC conference, which met in 1949 in Bloemfontein, the judicial capital of South Africa.

Here, the Youth League passed a vote of no confidence in the organization and proposed a nationwide stay-at-home from work on June 26, 1950. In order to assert their authority, the older members of the ANC announced their own date for a stay-away from work— May 1. Nelson advised them there was not enough time to plan for a safe, effective strike on that date. Nevertheless, the ANC went ahead with its plans. Without enough time and lacking proper organization, the stay-away resulted in many deaths and injuries, as Nelson had predicted.

After this failure, the ANC put Nelson Mandela in charge of organizing all future protests. This meant Nelson had to travel to all the provinces and be separated from his young family. With Mandela's legal expertise in even greater demand, he was earning enough money to support his family. Evelyn wanted to go to Durban in Natal Province to take a course in midwifery (delivering babies). Whenever Nelson visited Natal Province, usually to defend the ANC, he and Evelyn would be able to see each other, but these visits were very few.

Besides working with the ANC, Nelson was busy defending clients who had broken the apartheid laws. Often, the temptations of the city led young black men into the wrong crowd and away from traditions of close tribal ties. Oliver Tambo, Nelson's law partner, observed, "South African apartheid laws turn innumerable innocent people into 'criminals.' . . . Every case in court, every visit to the prison to interview clients, reminded us of the humiliation and suffering burning into our people."

The brutal treatment of Africans by the police enraged Nelson even more. When the white police were on patrol in the townships, they would snap their long rubber whips from the back of an open truck, striking innocent blacks at random. Those lashes left deep, bleeding wounds on their backs. The police were also known to use torture. They would arrest an African, place a water hose nozzle in his mouth, and turn on the water until the body bloated and burst.

To make the best use of his time, Nelson decided to open a law office in downtown Johannesburg with Oliver Tambo as his partner. They rented space in Chancellor House, owned by Indians. There on the second floor were the names "Mandela and Tambo."

Tambo recalled those early law days in 1952: "For years we worked side by side. To reach our desks each morning, Nelson and I ran the gauntlet of patient lines of people overflowing from chairs in the waiting room into the corridors. South Africa has the dubious reputation of boasting one of the highest prison populations in the world. Jails are jam-packed with Africans imprisoned—some for serious offenses, but many for petty infringements of statutory law that no really civilized society would punish with imprisonment."

In the years before 1961, Mandela continued to advise his people to remain peaceful in their public protests. Some members of the ANC wanted to take a more militant stand, but Tambo and Mandela remained moderating influences. They had been inspired by the peaceful movement for passive resistance used by the great Mohandas K. Gandhi in India against the British in 1946. In fact, Gandhi had come to South Africa in 1913 and 1914 as a young lawyer and had protested the treatment of Indians. Like Gandhi, Nelson's natural instinct was to avoid violence.

The ANC needed strong leadership, and in 1952 they chose a new president, Albert John Luthuli. Luthuli was an African chief from Zululand—a black territory north of Natal Province where six million blacks of the Zulu tribe lived. Because of his experience as a schoolteacher and a sometime minister, Luthuli was regarded as a wise man, worthy of respect. Nelson, too, was gaining a reputation as a gifted speaker and a good organizer, and he was elected to be Luthuli's deputy. Mandela also was elected to be president of the Transvaal section of the ANC. Together, Mandela and Luthuli traveled to the four provinces giving speeches.

Mandela speaks to a crowd in the early 1950s.

Luthuli's daughter, Tandi Gcabashe—now of the American Friends' Service Committee for South Africa in Atlanta, Georgia—recalled those days when Nelson Mandela came to her home to visit her father in Groutville in Natal Province. "My father found Nelson Mandela very trustworthy. He trusted him because of his very sharp mind and his analysis of issues. He liked his directness and his commitment to whatever he decided to do. I remember him as a very energetic young man and very clear in his thinking."

In 1952 the ANC decided to copy the Defiance

Campaign that had been tried successfully by the Indians of South Africa right after World War II. Nonviolent protests and strikes by Indians had proved effective. Therefore, the ANC and the Indian Congress joined forces, forming the Defiance of Unjust Laws Campaign to fight peaceably against South Africa's apartheid laws. This campaign gathered support from Africans, Indians, and Coloreds, giving the nonwhites a sense of unity.

Joining forces with the Indians was a significant step. For at least two centuries, Indians and black Africans had been rivals for better jobs in South Africa and had developed a dislike for each other. Until Nelson made friends with Indian law students at Witwatersrand University, he, too, had a cultural prejudice against South African Indians.

The ANC also wanted to work through proper legal channels. Therefore, Nelson wrote to Prime Minister Daniel F. Malan in January 1952 hoping to persuade him to do something about the unjust laws against all races. A brief and rude reply came back from the secretary, telling Nelson to write to the minister of Native Affairs—who was the unpopular and rigid Hendrik Verwoerd.

Ignoring this reply, Nelson went with Chief Luthuli to Port Elizabeth where 35,000 blacks were gathered to hear Luthuli speak as the new president of

Mandela (center) during the 1952 Defiance Campaign trial.

the ANC. When Luthuli and Mandela reached the Orange Free State for another round of talks, the South African police were waiting to hand them "banning orders." A banning order prevented a person from attending gatherings of more than three people would include Africans, Indians, Coloreds, trade unionists, and white liberals (from the Congress of Democrats). He suggested that a Freedom Charter, outlining the goals of the COP, be written. Mandela agreed with his proposals.

When the multiple banning orders for Mandela and Luthuli expired in 1955, they called a meeting for the Congress of People in Kliptown, an area southwest of Johannesburg, to which all races were invited. More than 3,000 people attended with the burly security police watching. The Freedom Charter, a Bill of Rights similar to that of the United States, was read. "We the people of South Africa declare for all our country and the world to know; that South Africa belongs to all who live in it, black and white, and that no government can justly claim authority unless it is based on the will of the people."

The consequences of the COP meeting would change Mandela's future. When the meeting was over, the police invaded the entire area and seized all the documents, some of which would be used as evidence against Mandela and others within 18 months.

Part of the backlash from this Freedom Charter meeting was the requirement that black women carry passes, too. This meant that women could be arrested as readily as men. Black women angrily protested to the new prime minister, Johannes G. Strijdom, who had taken over from Doctor Malan in 1955. Since the women received no response, 20,000 of them marched through the streets of Pretoria in October 1955, shouting slogans and singing songs. To conclude, they stood silently in front of the government buildings. But their protest was unavailing. In 1956 black women were forced by law to carry passes.

Amid all the political turmoil, Nelson Mandela's marriage to Evelyn was gradually coming to an end. Their separation and his many long absences had caused arguments and misunderstandings between them. In 1956 Nelson moved away from the home.

Not only was Nelson's personal life in turmoil, but so was his public life. The leading members of the ANC were under constant surveillance by the South African police as a result of the Kliptown meeting. Nelson's political career would go through troublesome times, but an unexpected new love would make his future tragedies bearable.

Chapter / Six

Treason Trial and Winnie

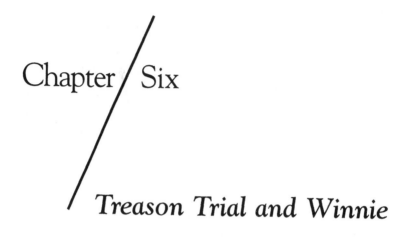

Night was never very safe for blacks in South Africa during the 1950s. They were always listening for the fists of the police pounding on their front doors anytime between midnight and dawn. But Nelson never felt this fear. He slept soundly for the few hours he needed. His children and relatives were more distressed than he was.

However, on a dark morning early in December of 1956, there was a loud knock on Nelson's door. He knew who it was—the police. As they gathered up all of his personal papers and documents, he was instructed to pack some things and come with them.

The government had become suspicious of the increasing unrest among Africans and Indians. After the Kliptown meeting, the government was convinced that the Freedom Charter was part of a Communist plot to start a revolution that would overthrow the white government. To stop the so-called plot, they arrested 156 of the key organizers from the Congress of People. These leaders were members from all races, including 23 whites. Joe Slovo, a lawyer and one of Mandela's friends, was one of them. The government decided to put them all on trial for treason under the Suppression of Communism Act. The code name for the sweep of arrests was "Operation T."

When the police drove Nelson, Walter Sisulu, and Oliver Tambo to the Fort Prison in Johannesburg, the three friends joined 153 other political prisoners who had been flown in from all over South Africa. They were all clearly connected to the Congress of People—the men and women from the now famous Kliptown rally where the Freedom Charter was introduced in 1955.

Once in jail, Nelson was amused that 156 supposedly dangerous people were crowded into two cells. They couldn't have been more pleased to be together, despite the physical discomfort. It was almost like a reunion, and they were able to talk seriously about their plans and beliefs. Mandela's booming laugh and quiet reasoning encouraged them.

When the trial began just before Christmas, there was a large demonstration outside the Drill Hall in Jo-

Mandela (right) arrives in Pretoria during the first treason trials, 1958.

hannesburg. A sympathetic crowd was waiting for the accused to arrive in police vans. A loud roar would go up as each familiar figure stepped out of the van. Although the crowd was peaceful, they sang songs and began a celebration dance called *toyi toyiing*. The police became nervous and fired at them, injuring 22 people.

As the pretrial hearings opened, the 156 defendants were placed in a cage inside the courtroom. To degrade the accused, someone had hung a sign on the cage, that said DON'T FEED. Angered, the defense lawyer persuaded the judge to let all of them out on bail to wait for the trial. A few stayed in Johannesburg with Nelson, who drove them from the township to the court each day. These preliminary hearings lasted nine months. Again, Nelson enjoyed the time with his children.

Because the treason trial would last from 1956 to 1961, many of the 156 on trial could not afford the legal fees. Nor could they commute to Johannesburg for the hearings while trying to earn a living and support their families. Sympathetic to their plight, a few key people in the white community came to their rescue. They were Bishop Ambrose Reeves of Johannesburg, who demanded equality for all people; Alex Hepple, a member of Parliament for the Labor Party; and Alan Paton, a Liberal Party member and international writer, famous for his novel, *Cry the Beloved Country*. These three formed a Defense and Aid Fund to help support the families of the accused.

In the preliminary hearings, the defense called upon Dr. Andrew Murray, a professor from the University of Cape Town. Doctor Murray was recognized by the government as an expert on communism and was asked to testify and identify a Communist by his writings. Without telling him the source, lawyers for the defense read him a passage from his own textbook. Upon hearing it, Murray stated that the author must be a Communist. As a result, the judge dismissed the charges against 65 of the accused, but 91 remained on trial.

While the treason trial dragged on, life for black Africans was worsening. In 1960 the bus companies in Johannesburg raised the cost of their fares. This was an explosive issue for Africans, who couldn't afford to pay any more out of their small paychecks. Thousands boycotted the buses, and 14,000 Africans were arrested in Alexandra township. In fact, 6,000 Africans walked to work each day, leaving home an hour or two earlier.

Eventually, the ANC agreed to accept a government subsidy as compensation for the higher bus fares. Some of the more militant members of the ANC thought this was a sellout, although it avoided violence and put people back to work.

Because the key organizers of the ANC were shuttling back and forth to the trial, the group was virtually leaderless. The ANC members had no one to direct them, inspire them, or organize them.

To fill the void, a wider organization came into being in 1959. It was called the Pan African Congress (PAC) with Robert Sobukwe, a university lecturer, elected as its chairman. The PAC became a political rival to the ANC. Nelson Mandela had great respect for Sobukwe and in fact had defended him in 1950, but he was disappointed at this new development.

The PAC wanted "Africa for the Africans" (black Africans) and they wanted independence by 1963. Mandela, however, wanted democracy for all races in South Africa—black and white. The PAC was involved in organizing trade unions and was opposed to whites making decisions for blacks in Parliament. Mandela, on the other hand, had suggested that 60 blacks could be selected to represent nonwhite views in Parliament. However, the birth and popularity of the PAC definitely weakened the ANC.

Although the treason trial limited his freedom and demanded much legal preparation, Nelson continued to see and spend time with his children. Because of the split in his marriage, he lived in Orlando West while Evelyn lived in Orlando East with their two sons and daughter. The children managed to see each parent during this time. (Evelyn eventually returned to a small village near Qunu in the Transkei where she worked in a country store. She did not remarry.)

Then, in the second year of the trial, something happened to change and brighten Nelson's life. One day in 1957, as he was buying a sandwich in a store in Johannesburg, his good friend Oliver Tambo drove by with his fiancée, Adelaide, and a friend of hers. Adelaide hopped out of the car and introduced

Winnie Madikizela to Nelson. Winnie was a tall, slim young woman in her early twenties with big, round brown eyes. She had heard of Nelson since her days in high school and smiled shyly at him. Nelson joined them on their way to drop Winnie at the hospital where she was employed as a social worker.

The next day, to Winnie's astonishment, Nelson called to ask her to have lunch with him. He sent a car, which brought her to his law office, and they went to an Indian restaurant. Eating spicy curry was a new experience for Winnie. Nelson was amused at the way she coughed and her eyes filled with tears from the highly seasoned food. After their meal, they drove into the country and walked, talking about their childhoods.

Although he was 16 years her elder, their backgrounds had some similarities. They were from neighboring tribes in the Transkei, Nelson from the Thembu tribe and Winnie from the Pondo tribe—both part of the larger Xhosa tribe. Winnie was only ten when her mother died, as Nelson had been when his father died. Winnie was also born to Methodist parents and attended Methodist schools, and she was very eager to continue her education into adult years. Winnie had completed her field studies in social work in the Transkei, near where Nelson had grown up. She had been shocked by the conditions of malnutrition and lack of medical aid. Like Nelson, she wanted to do what was best for her people. She was strong, mentally and physically. For what was ahead of them, this would be important.

When Winnie was born on September 26, 1936, her parents, Columbus and Gertrude Madikizela, were hoping for a boy. She was the fourth of nine children. Although her name was long—Nomzamo Zanyiwe Winifred Madikizela, they called her "girl." Not until she went to school was she called Winnie. However, the African part of her name meant "someone who would have trials." To please her parents, who were both schoolteachers, she tried to be better than her brothers in schoolwork and at play. She was.

Winnie never felt that she was different because of the color of her skin until the end of World War II. Her village celebrated the Allied victory in the town hall, but all blacks were barred from taking part in the festivities. Winnie peered sadly through the window at the small group of white people living in her village. They were laughing and eating inside. She noticed the different tone of voice used by the white man who owned the grocery store. He was much nicer to whites than to blacks.

Winnie attended Shawbury High School in Qumbu, which was some distance from her home in Bizana, East Pondoland. There, she studied with teachers from Fort Hare and became a popular but shy girl. During her last year there, many students were striking to show support for the Defiance Campaign in 1952. Because her father and sister had made sacrifices for her to come to this school, she didn't feel she could risk being expelled and so did not strike. Since the Bantu Education Act was passed the next year (1953), she might not have had the same educational opportunities if she had left school.

Finishing school with high marks in 1952, Winnie had to decide what to do next. Her father thought she should go to Johannesburg to study at a college that trained medical social workers. Frightened and timid, she boarded the train to Johannesburg and was met by two white girls from the Jan Hofmeyr School of Social Work. Like Nelson, she was dazzled by the liveliness of the city and shocked by the conditions in the townships, where she worked in hospitals.

When Winnie returned to the Transkei to help her people, her father could see that she was becoming a beautiful young woman. Without telling her, he began searching for a proper husband to form an arranged marriage. When Winnie found out, she packed her things and fled back to Johannesburg.

Because of her outstanding school record, Winnie was offered a scholarship to study in the United States. She was excited and proud, but torn between accepting that offer or becoming the first black medical social worker in South Africa. As much as she wanted to go to America, Winnie felt she could do the most good in her own country. By then she had met Nelson Mandela.

Nelson was very much in love with Winnie. It was obvious because he introduced her to his children, friends, and relatives, hoping to gain their approval. The children liked her, but many acquaintances in Qunu resented the breakup of his marriage and his new relationship with this younger woman. He never offered a formal proposal of marriage to Winnie. When his divorce from Evelyn became official in 1958, Nelson casually said in the car one day, "You should have your wedding gown made soon." That was the first Winnie had heard of marriage. But she did have the gown made.

The wedding was a grand occasion in Winnie's home village of Bizana on June 14, 1958. Nelson was able to persuade the authorities to give him four days' release from his banning order to get married. Before and after the Methodist ceremony, there were dances, songs, and gifts, in keeping with African tradition. There were feasts and a 14-tier wedding cake. (Also, part of the tradition was for Nelson to pay lobola in the form of cattle to the bride's family, but the number of cattle he offered was never revealed.)

Although Winnie's father thought Nelson's politics were too radical, he was proud to have him as a son-in-law. However, his parting words to his daughter were, "You have married the struggle—not the man." His words would prove to be true.

The treason trial dragged on as Nelson and Winnie started their married life. Winnie soon discovered that she was going to have a baby. In the early stages of her pregnancy, she joined the women's group of the ANC and protested against the extension of the pass law, which demanded that women carry passes. She was arrested and taken to the Johannesburg Fort, where all the women had to sleep on the floor, each on a grass mat and each with a smelly blanket. Fortunately, Albertina Sisulu, Walter Sisulu's wife, was able to help her in jail where she almost lost her baby.

The women were released from jail when the ANC paid all the fines for them. Because of her association with the ANC, Winnie lost her job at the hospital. But the birth of her baby, Zenani Mandela, on February 4, 1959, made up for that disappointment. When Zenani was five months old, Winnie found a job with the Johannesburg Child Welfare Department. Fortunately, there were two grandmothers to care for the baby because Winnie needed and wanted to work. For Nelson, still struggling with the treason trial, the difficulties of his life were offset by brief and

Winnie Mandela arrives outside the court in Pretoria in 1964. Mandela was about to be sentenced to life imprisonment. The woman on the left is Mandela's mother.

Mandela in 1958

treasured moments with his family and the advent in 1960 of a second daughter, Zindzi.

The treason trial stretched from months into years. Lack of rent money, lack of time, and the Group Areas Act forced Nelson and Oliver Tambo to give up their law office. Both continued to practice law unofficially in the townships, helping clients at night and on weekends.

Between 1956 and 1961, Nelson tried to explain to the judge and the court that he was not a Communist. In the old African societies everyone was free and equal. Because these societies were democratically run, he was influenced to believe in the system.

The prosecutor questioned Nelson closely about how he wanted to achieve democracy. Nelson frankly admitted that the ANC expected to use economic pressure to attain its demands for nonwhites. Nelson had realized that white people's need for black labor gave that labor more power than they realized. He suggested that the government and the ANC talk to find a way for blacks to be represented in Parliament. If that were achieved, Mandela promised to stop civil disobedience. In his testimony, Nelson said, "We shall have our people's democracy, my Lords. That is the view I hold—whether that is the Congress's view I don't know, but that is my view."

Chapter / Seven

Mandela Abandons Nonviolence

Sharpeville.

That name would echo around the world for years to come and would go down in history as one of the most horrifying moments in South African history.

On March 21, 1960, thousands of Africans did not go to work. Instead, they walked peacefully to police stations in suburbs outside Johannesburg and Cape Town. There, they stood and told the police, the government, and the world that the law forcing them to carry passes was unjust and unfair.

The Pan African Congress (PAC), under Robert Sobukwe, was the organizer of this Anti-Pass Day. Sobukwe had a dream for Africa. He wanted to make it all black (a Pan Africa) from Cape Town to Cairo (in contrast to Cecil John Rhodes's dream of making

Crowds gather at Sharpeville—before any shots were fired.

Africa British from Cape Town to Cairo). In fact, Sobukwe wanted a United States of black Africa. But Nelson Mandela knew this was unrealistic as long as apartheid held its grip on South Africa.

Using Gandhi's method of passive resistance, Sobukwe informed the commissioner of police that the members of the PAC would be coming and gave him their reason—opposition to the pass laws.

The police were waiting for them, heavily armed, although the Africans were empty-handed. As the 75 young South African policemen stood at attention, 5,000 Africans marched to the police station in Sharpeville township, 50 miles outside Johannesburg.

For several hours, the demonstrators stood in the hot sun. When anything happened behind the wire fence around the station, they surged forward in curiosity. Frightened by the masses of black people closing in on them, the young policemen suddenly fired their rifles, without orders. The protestors scattered in every direction, but in their wake, 69 were left dead and 180 were wounded. Most were shot in the back.

In Cape Town, thousands of Africans followed PAC member Philip Kgosana like a pied piper, from the townships of Nyanga and Langa to police headquarters in downtown Cape Town. Alarmed by the threat of violence in the heart of Cape Town, a brigadier promised Kgosana that the minister of justice would talk with him if Kgosana would tell his followers to go home peacefully. Philip was a university student and because of his youth he believed the brigadier's offer. When Philip announced through a megaphone that he would meet the minister of justice, the crowd cheered and returned to their homes. But the brigadier immediately broke his promise and arrested Philip. On his deathbed in 1990, that same brigadier confessed that he had carried the guilt of his broken promise for 30 years.

Only a month before Sharpeville, the prime minister of Great Britain, Harold Macmillan, had visited Cape Town and had spoken boldly about "the winds

Sharpeville—after police had fired at the crowd.

of change sweeping through Africa." He was referring to the 1957 independence of Ghana in West Africa and the breakaway from colonial rule in East Africa's Kenya. Now Macmillan denounced South Africa's racial policies in an address to Parliament. The address shocked President Verwoerd. Perhaps Sobukwe, too, thought Sharpeville would be another wind of change to start blowing in South Africa.

The world reacted with horror. The United Nations condemned what came to be known as the Sharpeville Massacre. The United States, with its own racial struggles, was horrified. Even the Dutch Parliament issued a statement of condemnation.

Many white South Africans were afraid that Sharpeville was to be the beginning of a bloody civil war. Some left the country for England and Australia. Others took a more sympathetic view toward the inhumane treatment of blacks. A group of white women, called the Black Sash women, stood silently in front of the Parliament Building in Cape Town to express their displeasure. Each woman wore a black sash draped from her shoulder to her waist, representing her mourning for those killed and wounded at Sharpeville.

Learning of these events while in Johannesburg, Nelson was heartsick. His faith in peaceful resistance and compromise began to crumble. Yet, he still felt that stay-at-home strikes were more effective than large public demonstrations, and they avoided violence.

As a result of Sharpeville and a falling stock market, the government called a state of emergency. Both the ANC and PAC were banned on April 30, 1960. No blacks were permitted on the streets after sundown, no public meetings were allowed, and the press was forbidden to print inflammatory stories. These were the factors that would soon change Mandela's mind about his future plans for the ANC.

Before the state of emergency went into effect, Oliver Tambo, who had been banned for another five years but was out on bail for the treason trial, decided to escape into Botswana, a country north of South Africa. As president of the ANC, Tambo felt he could do more good in exile than in jail for years. He traveled from Botswana to Tanzania to West Africa and eventually to London, gaining support for the ANC.

Because the ANC was now banned in South Africa and Tambo could not reenter the country legally, he established the headquarters of the ANC in Lusaka, Northern Rhodesia (now Zambia).

But Mandela decided to make another kind of protest. Mandela, Chief Luthuli, and Duma Nokwe (a lawyer and secretary general of the ANC) burned their passes to the cheers of residents of Orlando

West, Mandela's township. The police stormed Orlando, arrested the three men, and took them to prison in Pretoria. Any of the treason trial defendants who were out on bail were also rounded up, as well as 2,000 black "troublemakers."

Mandela and the others were squeezed into a series of small cells. The conditions and food were dreadful. A bucket served as a toilet for five people in each cell. The floor mats and blankets had lice in them. Food was a watery oatmeal porridge. Nelson acted as spokesman for the prisoners and complained about the food. His guards threatened him and ignored his complaint.

However, when Nelson appeared in court, he made a public plea to the judge. "Speaking with the greatest moderation, it is no exaggeration to say that the food which is furnished to us in jail, my Lord, with due respect, is completely unfit for human consumption." An investigation was ordered by the judge, and the food soon improved.

Meanwhile, the treason trial continued. The judge had many questions for Nelson about the attitude of blacks toward whites. Again and again Nelson answered, "We are not antiwhite. We are against white supremacy . . . and we have condemned racialism no matter by whom it is professed." Again Nelson was asked about communism and again he denied being a member of the Communist party. However, Mandela mentioned that he was impressed with the Soviet Union because it had no color bar.

When the state of emergency was lifted and Mandela had completed giving his evidence in the treason trial at the end of August 1960, he was released from prison and returned to the arms of his wife and children although still under a banning order. Before he could enjoy their company, he heard that his son in the Transkei was dangerously ill. Defying his banning order, he drove all night to see the boy and brought him back to Johannesburg for treatment.

In the spring of 1961, the final arguments for the treason trial were heard. The government was reluctant to see the powerful organizers of the ANC released, even though most of the 156 had already been cleared of any wrongdoing. Now, however, there remained only two dozen, including Nelson, who had to await their verdict. By this time, their white lawyer, Bram Fischer, had submitted over 400 pages of evidence.

The judge's words rang in Nelson's ears. "You are found not guilty and discharged. You may go." Hoisting Bram Fischer on their shoulders, Nelson and his friends rushed outside into the March air as free men. For five years, Nelson Mandela had either been under banning orders or on trial. Now, he was free.

Determined but free, Mandela is acquitted in 1961.

While black Africans were struggling to establish freedom within their own country, white Afrikaners were unhappy with their ties to Great Britain. The Commonwealth countries criticized South Africa's racial policies at a conference in London in 1961. Reacting angrily to British interference, Pres. Hendrik Verwoerd and his government decided that on May 31, 1961, South Africa would no longer be the Union of South Africa—a dominion of the British Commonwealth—but the Republic of South Africa—a nation independent of Britain.

The idea of a republic without democracy for all races was appalling to Nelson. Although the ANC was outlawed, its leaders planned to hold a conference of 1,400 delegates in Pietermaritzburg, near Durban, at the end of March 1961.

For the first time in many years Mandela was free without a banning order. Therefore, he was able to appear as the main speaker at the convention. He spoke because he felt that the blacks had to put on record their feelings about a republic that did not recognize the rights of the majority of the population.

In clear and strong words, he said, "Now that the ANC, which has been the sword and shield of the African people for 50 years, has been suppressed, it has two alternatives: either to accept discrimination and humiliation or stand firm for its rights. We can stand disunited in the face of the government's arrogance, or we can stand united to ensure that the government's discriminatory legislation does not work." The delegates stood and applauded.

From this moment on, Nelson Mandela's personal life changed. A National Action Council was formed to organize labor strikes in the country, in particular a three-day strike at the time South Africa would become a republic. The Council and the names of its members were to be kept secret to avoid arrest. Nelson would be the head of the Council, but his name would not be secret. To escape future bannings and possible arrest, Nelson worked underground.

That last day at his home in Orlando West, his closest colleagues gathered around him. Nelson had been quiet the last few days at home. He had not told Winnie of his decision. Now, he turned to her and said, "Darling, just pack some of my clothes in a suitcase with my toiletries. I will be going away for a long time. You're not to worry, my friends here will look after you. They'll give you news of me from time to time. Look well after the children. I know you'll have the strength and courage to do so without me. I now know you are capable of that."

Winnie already knew he was going. In his shirt pocket she had found a receipt for six months' rent paid in advance.

As Nelson disappeared into a life of hiding, he was nicknamed the "Black Pimpernel." The name came from a famous novel about the French Revolution, in which a man called the Scarlet Pimpernel wore many disguises and escaped from his captors through back windows and by hiding in sewers and basements. Mandela did the same. These wild tales of outwitting the police gave Nelson the aura of a romantic figure. He was protected by sympathetic whites, blacks, and Indians. At night, he came out of hiding to conduct secret ANC meetings or to call newspapers from telephone booths to give them news for their front pages.

Mandela was on the run for more than a year, leaving hardly a trail for the police. Only rarely did Winnie hear that special family knock at the door to find her giant husband standing there, wearing that Mandela smile. Sometimes they met in cars or at friends' houses. Other times, he was disguised as a street cleaner or chauffeur. Often, she did not recognize him. Wherever it was, their time together was all too short.

Because Nelson felt he had no other choice, he told the judge in the treason trial, "I have had to separate myself from my dear wife and children, from my mother and sisters, to live as an outlaw in my own land. I have had to close my business, to abandon my profession, and live in poverty and misery, as many of my people are doing. I shall fight the government side by side with you, inch by inch, mile by mile, until victory is won . . . nor will I surrender. The struggle is my life. I will continue fighting for freedom until the end of my days."

Here was the core of Nelson Mandela's life—the struggle. He was prepared to sacrifice his family for it. They understood and were ready for the heartaches that went with it. "I had so little time to love him and that love has survived all these years of separation," Winnie wrote later.

Unfortunately, the strike in May 1961 was not very successful. This time, the police were prepared. They had tapped the telephones of journalists and certain ANC members, and with promises of money and immunity, the authorities were paying informants. Meetings were banned. The police had seized printing presses and arrested 10,000 blacks. Furthermore, the military was working alongside the police.

Despite police threats, the May Day strikers in some areas stayed home one or two days, but not three. In other areas, people were afraid to strike at all. At this point, Mandela called off the strike.

Mandela later admitted in the trial, "It could not be denied that our policy to achieve a nonracial state by nonviolence had achieved nothing, and that our followers were beginning to lose confidence in this policy and were developing disturbing ideas of terrorism against whites . . . it was precisely because the soil of South Africa is already drenched with the blood of innocent Africans that we felt it our duty to make preparations as a long-term policy to use force in order to defend ourselves against force."

Chief Luthuli, who had always been a pacifist, was awarded the Nobel Peace Prize early in December 1961 for his tireless efforts in keeping the protests nonviolent. Two weeks later bombs began exploding throughout South Africa. Unbeknownst to Luthuli, Nelson—backed by most of the ANC leaders—had formed the *Umkhonto we Sizwe*, called the MK for short. (*Umkhonto we Sizwe* means "Spear of the Nation.") This militant arm of the ANC had been fully instructed in the art of sabotage to bomb buildings in the major cities. Railroad stations, factories, and some government buildings were targeted. In his heart, Nelson preferred nonviolence, but that had not worked to change the attitude of the government. Although Nelson insisted that white people should not be killed, inevitably some were. Once the sabotage campaign was underway, the search for Mandela intensified.

In the meantime, the ANC elected Mandela to represent them at a Pan African Freedom Movement conference in Ethiopia for delegates from South, Central, and East Africa, scheduled to meet in February 1962.

Dressed in a khaki uniform and using the assumed name of David Motsamai, Nelson escaped into Botswana one January night in 1962. To breathe the air of freedom and not have to worry about looking over his shoulder was a new experience for him.

The first stop on Nelson's way to Ethiopia was in Tanganyika (now Tanzania) where he met with black Prime Minister Julius Nyere. From there, he went to Lagos, Nigeria, where he joined Oliver Tambo.

Nelson and Oliver went directly to the capital of Ethiopia, Addis Ababa, for the eight-day conference with black officials from all over Africa. There they celebrated their anticipated freedom from colonialists. Many of the speeches attacked Belgians for colonizing the Belgian Congo (Zaire); the Portuguese for colonizing Mozambique and Angola; and the Boers for holding South Africa in chains.

When it was time for Nelson to give a speech, he was introduced as David Motsamai from South Africa. A curious hush fell over the audience as the tall Mandela strode to the platform. Before launching into his address, he reintroduced himself as Nelson Mandela. He received a standing ovation. He thanked them and said that he spoke on behalf of

Chief Luthuli, Oliver Tambo, and all black Africans
in South Africa in seeking their moral support. His
speech had been approved and edited by Tambo and
other key members of the ANC. "South Africa is now
a land ruled by the gun," he said.

Once Mandela abandoned his disguise, reporters
told the world of his whereabouts. But the South African police had a difficult time tracking his political
path from Libya and Cairo to the cluster of independent countries on the bulge of West Africa: Mali,
Guinea, Sierra Leone, Liberia, Ghana, and the countries on the lip of North Africa: Tunisia, Morocco,
and Algeria. Mandela even left the African continent
for Great Britain where he met with leaders of the Labor and Liberal parties, asking for their support and
help.

Tambo and Mandela would crisscross Africa,
seeking money and military training for ANC members outside South Africa. If black Africans had to
fight for their rights, they were prepared to wage
guerilla war. Mandela reluctantly came to believe
more and more that passive resistance would not bring
freedom to his people.

When July 1962 came, Nelson had completed his
assignment. He had raised money for the ANC, arranged for military training for young men of the
ANC in Ethiopia and a few West African countries,

and was now ready to return to his homeland.

When Mandela secretly crossed into South Africa wearing a disguise, he was saddened. For six months he had walked as a free man. He had watched sunsets and he had witnessed free discussions in London's House of Commons without fear. "Free from white oppression, from the idiocy of apartheid and racial arrogance, from police molestation, from humiliation and indignity. Wherever I went I was treated like a human being. In the African states I saw black and white mingling peacefully and happily in hotels, cinemas: trading in the same areas, using the same public transport, and living in the same residential areas," he said.

Now he was returning to apartheid. For him, there was no other choice. He would not abandon Winnie and his children or the cause of freedom for his people.

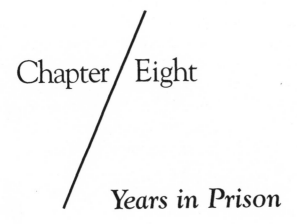

Chapter / Eight

Years in Prison

On a dark night in July 1962, Mandela crossed back into his own country, once again a prisoner to apartheid. His return was risky, for he had broken the law both by leaving South Africa illegally and by representing the ANC, which was still banned two years after Sharpeville.

In his absence, his wife and children had been subjected to many nightly raids at their home. Hoping to catch Mandela or to frighten Winnie into revealing where he was, the police shouted and waved their guns in a threatening way.

To avoid these police traps, Nelson went deeper into hiding upon his return. A white couple, Arthur and Hazel Goldreich, owned a farm, called Lillieslief, in the white section of Rivonia outside Johannesburg.

Here, in one of the cottages on the spacious grounds, Nelson was reunited with his family. Within the safety of the farm, Nelson played and laughed with Makgatho, his son from his first marriage, and his growing daughters.

This farm in Rivonia would become the underground headquarters of the militant *Umkhonto we Sizwe*, where sabotage attempts were planned for targets throughout South Africa. Many political activists in the ANC and in the South African Communist Party (SACP), under the leadership of Joe Slovo, met there in secret.

But Nelson would not stay there too long. He wanted to see Chief Luthuli and others to report on the fruits of his trip. This time, he disguised himself as a chauffeur for a theater director, Cecil Williams, who was sympathetic to his cause.

On Sunday morning, August 5, 1962, Nelson was driving Williams from Durban to Johannesburg when several police cars came from behind and stopped them. The disguise of David Motsamai did not fool them. They knew he was Nelson Mandela. Years later, in 1990, there was an unconfirmed story that someone who worked for the CIA had informed the South African police of Mandela's disguise and where they could find him. At that time, the CIA was convinced that the ANC was a Communist organization and, therefore, a threat to South Africa's stability. The accusation of a connection between the ANC and communism could be made because a number of white Communists such as Joe Slovo and Helen Joseph (a close friend of the Mandelas) were supportive members of the ANC.

Winnie learned the news of her husband's capture from one of his friends, who came to her place of work in the Child Welfare offices. "I knew that this was the end of any kind of family life, as was the case with millions of my people—I was no exception. Part of my soul went with him at that time."

Nelson Mandela was taken briefly to a jail in Pietermaritzburg before being transferred to a Johannesburg jail early in August 1962. On August 8, he was charged with leaving the country illegally and with directing the May Day strikes in 1961. Shortly thereafter, the banning orders became stricter on sympathetic whites as well as nonwhites. Helen Joseph was put under house arrest, as was Walter Sisulu. House arrest meant that one couldn't leave one's home or have more than one visitor at a time. Telephone calls could be received from relatives, but were recorded by the police.

On October 22, Mandela was scheduled to appear in court, this time in Pretoria instead of Johannesburg. Nelson's lawyer was Joe Slovo. However, Nel-

Winnie Mandela arrives at court on October 22, 1962.

son told the court that he would have to defend himself because Slovo, who was under a banning order,
could not leave Johannesburg to represent him in
Pretoria. To prepare his defense, Nelson requested a
lamp, a chair, and a table for his cell. Despite his eloquent self-defense, Nelson Mandela was declared
guilty on October 25.

On the day of sentencing (November 7), the
courtroom was filled with black supporters, shouting
"*Amandla!*" ("power"). Much to the displeasure of court
officials, Mandela wore his tribal costume, a leopard
kaross (a type of African toga), throughout the trial.
After the judge listed Mandela's offenses, Nelson
spoke for 70 minutes, impressing listeners.

"I hoped that life might offer me the opportunity
to serve my people and make my own humble contri-
bution to their freedom struggle. That is what has
motivated me in all that I have done. . . . Basically
we fight against two features which are the hallmarks
of African life in South Africa . . . poverty and lack
of human dignity . . . the direct result of the policy
of white supremacy," he told the judge.

After a ten-minute recess, the judge delivered
Nelson's sentence. Standing straight, Mandela
listened as the judge read what his future would be:
three years in jail for incitement (stirring up trouble)
and two years for going out of the country unlaw-

fully—a total of five years. Showing very little emotion, Mandela left the courtroom, smiling bravely.

Ironically, the United Nations condemned the system of apartheid on November 6, 1962, the day before Nelson's sentencing, and voted in favor of economic sanctions, calling for international businesses to withdraw their investments and suggesting a ban on the sale of certain imported products to South Africa.

While Mandela was imprisoned, the authorities tried to make him take off his tribal clothes and wear the prison uniform of khaki shorts and shirt. He refused. He also refused to eat the food. For this kind of resistance, he was put into solitary confinement for two months and allowed only 30 minutes each day in the open air.

Of that experience he said, "An hour was like a year. I was locked up in a bare cell, literally with nothing, nothing to read, nothing to write, nothing to do, and no one to talk or turn to. . . . I suffered the isolation for two months and finally concluded that nothing was more dehumanizing than isolation from human companionship."

Reluctantly, he accepted the uniform and the food. Among the prisoners at Pretoria Central Prison was Robert Sobukwe, the PAC leader of Sharpeville fame, who offered Nelson some suggestions on how to survive in prison.

Robben Island, Mandela's prison home until 1982. Cape Town and Table Island are seven miles away.

As sabotage sorties continued, Mandela was transferred from Pretoria Central Prison to Cape Town. There, he and other political prisoners were taken to Robben Island, a 300-year-old fortress within view of Cape Town's harbor. As the wooden boat rocked and bucked through the choppy waters for 45 minutes, Nelson saw the gray walls rise up out of the sea through a thick mist. A southeaster was blowing. Nelson and his fellow prisoners would come to know the signs of bad weather.

Here, his first work assignment was to crush rocks

for gravel. The warders were rough with the prisoners.
The icy waters were treacherous and offered no hope
of escape. For months, Nelson was not allowed to see,
hear from, or write to anyone. Finally, he was permitted to write 500 words to Winnie every six months.
Eventually, visits that lasted 30 minutes were granted
twice a year.

Meanwhile, Winnie was coping with the absence
of her husband and the prospect of being alone for five
years. For her children, she had to be brave, and she
taught them not to cry—tears were a sign of weakness.
She herself had been issued a two-year banning order
in January of 1962 and had lost her job. When she
placed her daughters in a school for Coloreds, the police ordered them suspended since they were not Colored, but African. Finally, through the help of a British couple at Witwatersrand University, Zenani and
Zindzi were sent to boarding schools in Swaziland, a
Commonwealth country in the northeast corner of
South Africa. Except for vacations at home, they were
not subjected to the turbulent life of bannings, imprisonment, and police harassment that their mother
experienced.

Reacting to the more than 200 incidents of sabotage since Nelson's sentencing, the police cracked
down on the ANC and the South African Communist
Party. Suspects were placed on 90-day detention un-

der the Suppression of Communism Act. Informants told the police about the house and cottages on the farm in Rivonia, Mandela's hiding place and the underground headquarters for *Umkhonto we Sizwe,* where the militant operations were being masterminded.

In July 1963 a sweep of the farm in Rivonia brought mass arrests, including those of Walter Sisulu and eight other key leaders. Sisulu had gone underground early in 1963 after many bannings and the threat of a six-year prison sentence. However, he was found guilty and sentenced to 26 years in prison. Arthur Goldreich was arrested, too, but somehow he managed to escape from prison.

Nelson Mandela's name was found among the documents that the police confiscated at Rivonia. He was taken from Robben Island and sent back to Pretoria for the Rivonia trial. Under the Suppression of Communism Act, Mandela and the other nine were accused of plotting to overthrow the government through violence.

Once again, Nelson Mandela took the witness stand and impressed his courtroom listeners with his forthrightness. He had lost 40 pounds and his appearance shocked those who knew him. Prison rations of porridge, bread, and watery soup were not nutritious. However, the air of dignity and confidence that

Mandela possessed was still there.

In his testimony, he traced every historic detail of *Umkhonto we Sizwe* and its relationship to the ANC. Nelson had not participated in those acts of terrorism, but as leader of *Umkhonto*, he was charged with them.

"The ideological creed of the ANC is and always has been the creed of African Nationalism," said Nelson. He defended the Freedom Charter, which he had sponsored in 1955 at the Kliptown meeting. " . . . the Freedom Charter is by no means a blueprint for a Socialist state. It calls for redistribution, but not nationalization of land. . . . It is true that there has often been close cooperation between the ANC and the Communist party. But cooperation is merely proof of a common goal—in this case the removal of white supremacy—and is not proof of a complete community of interests."

On June 11, 1964, the verdict was passed on Mandela and his colleagues. Many were expecting the death sentence.

The court waited silently for the decision. "The sentence is life imprisonment on all counts for the accused." Winnie's eyes filled with tears. A normal life with her husband was gone forever. But at least, he would live.

Chief Albert Luthuli, usually an even-tempered man, issued a strong press statement after the Rivonia decision. "I appeal to all governments throughout the world, to people everywhere, to organizations and institutions in every land and at every level, to act now to impose such sanctions on South Africa that will bring about the vital necessary change and avert what can become the greatest African tragedy of our times."

Not long afterward, the ten prisoners were flown directly to Robben Island.

For the next ten years, Nelson Mandela would do the same thing every day: wake up at 5:30 A.M., eat breakfast, work in the lime quarry pit until 4:30, eat dinner, and return to his cell. Sometimes he arose even earlier to go through a routine of exercises.

The political prisoners were kept separate and in solitary cells. At first, they were not let out for exercise, and they were not permitted to talk to each other. This deadly routine was made bearable because of the secret comradeship among the men. They had hidden snatches of conversation about politics, life, art, books, and families. The sound of hammering covered their bits of conversation. Mandela would often think up a historical question, which was whispered from prisoner to prisoner. The answers would be passed back to him. While working in the lime pit under a scorching sun, they sang tribal songs to make the time go by and help them forget their aching bodies. These songs at first were forbidden, but Mandela made a reasonable and eloquent, but firm, request. He finally succeeded in getting the ban against talking lifted.

Because Mandela and other political leaders were locked in cells in a separate section of the prison, exchange of information among the prisoners was limited. The only way to get and pass information was through the prison hospital. Here, gossip, complaints, and news were exchanged and taken back to the cells.

Mandela taught other prisoners not to respond to any verbal or physical ill-treatment by the warders. Instead, they would wait until the guards placed charges against them. At that point, they could defend themselves in front of a group of officials. If they followed Mandela's advice, most times the prisoners won. The guards discovered that when they treated the prisoners as gentlemen, there wasn't any trouble.

"The worst part of imprisonment is being locked up by yourself. You come face-to-face with time and there is nothing more terrifying than to be alone with sheer time. Then the ghosts come crowding in. They can be very sinister, very mischievous, raising a thousand doubts in your mind about the people outside, their loyalty. Was your sacrifice worth the trouble? What would your life have been like if you hadn't got involved?" explained Mandela.

Robben Island became known as "Mandela University." He encouraged young and old alike to study at night in their cells—to finish high school or start university courses.

In fact, Walter Sisulu and Nelson Mandela were considered father figures. Many came to them with their problems and for comfort. Since the prison authorities had respect for Mandela, he handled most of the complaints and arranged for library privileges.

Another occasional visitor who brought Mandela news was Helen Suzman. For more than 35 years, Mrs. Suzman was considered the only spokesperson for nonwhites in Parliament as a member of the Progressive Party until it became the Progressive Federal Party in 1977. "What I did was to voice opinions and make objections that coincided with the views of Africans, Coloreds, and Indians. I had a forum as a member of Parliament and a good deal of press publicity," she said.

From 1967 onward, Suzman saw Mandela eight or nine times on Robben Island. "Nelson Mandela was a man of great dignity under prison conditions. He spoke openly and courageously concerning the complaints made by prisoners about conditions. I took the complaints back to the ministers and gradually things got better. Study was considered a privilege and not a right, but eventually, the prisoners were given library and sports facilities. Most importantly, over the last ten years, the prisoners were allowed to get newspapers. Mandela was clearly the leader, and the prison authorities learned to treat him with a great deal of respect," said Mrs. Suzman.

Understandably, the prisoners of Robben Island yearned for the few visits from friends and relatives, who came from all over South Africa to see their loved ones. Before 1978 visitors had to sleep in train stations, on benches, and behind garbage cans to catch the ferry going out to the island. Some came year after year and missed the ferry's departure. After 1978 a small Anglican monastery, named Cowley House, was bought for the purpose of housing relatives of political prisoners and giving them free food and lodging the night before visiting Robben Island. These mothers, fathers, brothers, sisters, wives, and children were fearful and excited before the visits, but depressed afterward—not knowing when and if they would see their loved ones again.

Once on the island, police with dogs guided them to visitation rooms. Most visits were 15 to 30 minutes and were without physical contact—even an affectionate hug.

Weather was an important factor to prisoners on visiting days. Bad weather could cancel a visit that had been planned for six months to a year. A black poet, D. M. Moisi, wrote from his cell,

On the whims of wet weather my visits depend
When the sea's monstrous muscles swell,
My loved-ones with sore hearts home shall return
When clouds their smiling faces show,
Through the glass partition warm kisses I blow.

Nelson Mandela, too, longed for visits from Winnie. From 1964 to 1967, he had seen Winnie only three times. When his youngest daughter, Zindzi, was allowed to visit her father with Winnie, she felt she was intruding on an intimate moment. According to a close family friend, Helen Joseph, Zindzi had told her, "The love poured out of the eyes of my mother and father as they looked and talked with each other."

To occupy himself, Nelson studied for a London law degree. He also came to appreciate every glimpse of nature that he saw from his prison window or the prison yard. When his work duty wasn't in the lime pit, it was occasionally on the rocky banks of the island where he pulled seaweed. The sky, the water, the sea gulls, and the hazy outline of Table Mountain in the distance lifted his heart and gave him hope.

Sad news of Chief Luthuli's death came to Mandela in 1967. Luthuli was reportedly hit by a train while walking. According to a recent statement by Luthuli's daughter, this was untrue. "There were no multiple injuries, except for one big gash of a wound at the back of his head, which the family assumed was caused by a blow from an iron rod. He had just stepped off the train. In those days, the trains were run by coal, and the driver always carried an iron rod. We suspect he was assassinated by government agents."

In 1968 Nelson's mother died. It wasn't until several months later that Winnie was permitted to visit and tell Nelson of the funeral in the Transkei, which she attended.

Nelson's son by Evelyn, Thembi, was killed in a car accident in the Transkei in 1969. There couldn't have been a greater personal blow than the loss of his own child. Nelson is said to have spent that day alone in his cell to grieve.

Meanwhile, Winnie's life was full of ups and downs. She would be the victim of arrests, torture, house arrest, and a five-year banning order as well as six months in jail. Over a period of ten years, she would be robbed and threatened, which caused Nelson great anguish and frustration. In between these periods, she held temporary jobs as a social worker, a clerk, and a debt collector.

Because of Nelson's long imprisonment, many members of the ANC looked to Winnie as a substitute leader for her husband and a spokesperson for the ANC, which earned her the title of "Mother of the Nation." Committed to women and to education, Winnie joined the Federation for Black Women and the Black Parents' Association.

In 1976 the government insisted that Afrikaans, instead of English, should be the language used to teach all subjects in African schools. The reaction was explosive. Teachers didn't know the language, neither did their students. Parents were distressed.

The students themselves decided to protest by organizing a large rally in Soweto township. The police were there to see that it didn't get out of control. However, the tide of 15,000 black youngsters marching through Soweto frightened the police. They fired into the heart of the crowd, killing a young boy. Pictures of the dead youngster flashed around the world, horrifying readers and viewers everywhere. The world remembered, too well, the slaughter at Sharpeville 16 years earlier. Schools were closed and more demonstrations followed for a year, resulting in over 500 dead and close to 3,000 injured.

The South African police banned Winnie Mandela for encouraging the riot. But banning wasn't strong enough. They decided to load up her furniture in 1977 and move her, together with her daughter Zindzi, to Brandfort, a small town in the middle of the Orange Free State. Living conditions were primitive and Winnie demanded running water in her house. Eventually, the authorities gave in and ran a pipeline to her kitchen.

When the South African government insisted that Afrikaans should be taught in all schools, students and adults in Soweto protested. The result was a massacre in which more then 500 people were killed.

Her instincts as a social worker were aroused during her eight years of banishment in Brandfort. She opened a makeshift medical clinic in her house, helped the homeless, taught black women how to plant a vegetable garden, and sew their clothes.

After Sharpeville and the Soweto riot, another shock registered around the world. That was the brutal beating to death of Steve Biko in 1977 by the South African police. Biko, a soft-spoken and intelligent young black man from Port Elizabeth, was the leader of the Black Consciousness Movement, which had grown out of the black South African Students' Organization. Black Consciousness was a revolt against segregated universities for blacks and against the teaching of Afrikaans in the Bantu schools. Donald Woods, a white editor of a Port Elizabeth newspaper, had been a good friend of Biko's and supported his cause. The police hounded Woods because of his newspaper's editorials in support of Biko and because of his personal relationship to him. He fled the country with his family before they could arrest him. The Biko/Woods story was portrayed in a 1987 film called *Cry Freedom*.

Though Mandela could not act as a father in person, he wrote his children many letters from his prison cells, giving them advice, expressing his displeasure if they had done something wrong, and always letting them know of his deep love for each one of them.

Maki, his daughter from his first marriage, married against his advice when she was only 16. After the birth of her two children, she was divorced.

Nelson wrote to her in 1978 to say, "Divorce may destroy a woman, but strong characters have not only survived but gone further and distinguished them-

By the middle and late 1980s, many people were asking for Mandela's release from prison.

A typical cell in Pollsmoor Prison

selves in life. . . . I must ask you to think carefully about your future and to aim a little higher than you are doing now. Think, Maki, think, you are only twenty-four and the whole world is at your feet. Do not miss the chance of entering university next year."

From 1979 onward, Nelson Mandela, while remaining in prison, received honorary degrees and awards from around the world. Many countries petitioned South Africa for Mandela's release. International pressure and economic sanctions were placed on South Africa. Many nations reacted loudly and impatiently against apartheid and against the continued imprisonment of Nelson Mandela. At great personal risk, Desmond Tutu (an Anglican bishop of Johannesburg) and others courageously waged a "Free Mandela" campaign in 1980.

During Mandela's long years in prison, there were many changes in the political landscape of South Africa. In 1966 the rigid and steely Prime Minister Hendrik F. Verwoerd was assassinated in Parliament by a white man who worked as a messenger to members. Verwoerd's successor was J. B. Vorster, also a fanatical supporter of apartheid. By the time P. W. Botha was elected in 1978, there were signs of change. Botha would give hope to the ANC and the world.

For unstated reasons, in 1982 Mandela and the key members of ANC, including Walter Sisulu, were moved to Pollsmoor Prison in Cape Town. After Mandela's 1990 release, a legal adviser to the Mandelas explained the reason for the transfer to Pollsmoor. Apparently, Mandela had developed too strong a power base on Robben Island.

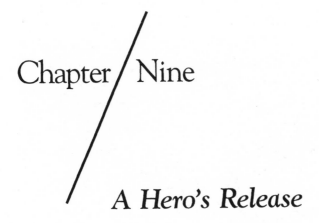

Chapter / Nine

A Hero's Release

Pollsmoor Prison is a sallow yellow brick structure that sits in the middle of a flat valley of grape vineyards. In the distance, a slate blue range of mountains rises as a backdrop to the vineyards and faces the ocean on the foreshore. Only from the Pollsmoor tower can one see the scenery above the severe prison cells and the enclosed prison yards.

Here, Nelson Mandela would spend six years, from 1982 to 1988. His constant companion would be Lieutenant Gregory, a round, kindly faced man, who was Mandela's prison warder for 22 years. Gregory had been transferred with Mandela from Robben Island to Pollsmoor and later to Victor Verster Prison, an hour's drive outside Cape Town.

In Pollsmoor, Mandela and others would come to

miss the fresh air and companionship of Robben Island. But here, he would see his wife and family more frequently. On one visit in 1984, Winnie was told by Officer Gregory that she would be allowed to have her first physical contact with her husband. For the first time in 22 years, Winnie and Nelson Mandela embraced each other. They were allowed two minutes.

Outside the prison, black politics was still smoldering. By 1983, 600 separate organizations were uniting into one political bloc, called the United Democratic Front (UDF) with Mandela as a patron. Many groups from churches to students united against apartheid. The UDF was governed by a committee of three, including Albertina Sisulu. Although it later lost its influence, the UDF was a strong voice in the 1980s. The purpose of the organization was to achieve "one man, one vote." Also, it campaigned for the release of Mandela.

For the whites, though, South Africa in the 1980s seemed to be under a reign of terror. Bombs had been set off in buildings—newspaper offices and radio stations being the main targets. In their homes, whites locked themselves behind their walls and gates. The radical blacks (*Umkhonto we Sizwe*) and the radical whites (AWB—an Afrikaner resistance movement led by Eugene TerreBlanche) were both to be feared. The *Umkhonto* wanted the government to move faster

Bombings to offices of anti-apartheid groups were common occurrences in the 1980s.

in uprooting apartheid, and the AWB whites wanted the government to stop all changes. Security police were everywhere, inspecting bags and people for explosives.

In 1982 more bomb attacks occurred throughout South Africa. This time, members of *Umkhonto* were killing and injuring both blacks and whites. Mandela in prison and Oliver Tambo in London opposed this violence.

The causes for unrest in 1984 had to do with the long drought in the homelands and the increase in rents within black townships where people simply couldn't pay any more. Before P. W. Botha was elected as president in 1985, he proposed some reformist policies. One such proposal was a tricameral type of parliament, in which the Coloreds, Indians, and whites would have direct representation, but the black Africans were ignored. Their homelands were supposed to serve as indirect representation for all blacks. To the outsider, this sounded like an improvement. But once again blacks were left out. The reaction among blacks was explosive. There were demonstrations and protests against the election for this new parliament. The election was boycotted by blacks, who represented 80 percent of the eligible voters.

Despite Botha's reluctance to deal with blacks, his minister of justice, Kobie Coetzee, had a secret but historic relationship with Nelson Mandela. From 1985, without fanfare and without the knowledge of the press, the two men met frequently. Several times, when Mandela was hospitalized for possible pneumonia or tuberculosis, Coetzee, unnoticed, visited him there.

Even while Mandela was in jail, the minister had Mandela brought to his home in Cape Town where they could talk about the political and racial future of South Africa. "I never saw Mr. Mandela behind bars.

President P. W. Botha

I saw him at my home. He is a man of integrity and intelligence—a man of old-world values. I am a lawyer and a student of history. I saw him in the hospital several times without the press knowing. It would have been political suicide for both of us. We are two lawyers. He is loyal to the ANC, and I expect him to be. Any decisions or actions I took were professional," said Mr. Coetzee in 1990. That final remark probably meant that any decisions he made about Nelson Mandela's release or any recommendations about the future of blacks in South Africa were based on his judgment as a lawyer and historian and not on his personal feelings about blacks. Apparently, Mandela and Coetzee had a very cordial and warm relationship.

Beginning in 1985, President P. W. Botha had enough political vision to initiate some improvements in the system of apartheid.

The first sign of moderation in the South African government came in 1985. Botha offered to release all those connected with the Rivonia trial. As the Rivonia spokesman, Mandela carefully considered this offer but then rejected it for all of them. His reasons were spelled out in a written document, which his daughter Zindzi read before 10,000 Africans gathered in a Soweto stadium.

Briefly, Mandela insisted on five conditions before the Rivonia prisoners would agree to leave prison. The government must renounce violence against blacks, dismantle apartheid, lift the ban on the ANC, free all political prisoners, and guarantee free political activity.

"Only free men can negotiate. Prisoners cannot enter into contracts. . . . Your freedom and mine cannot be separated. I will return (to prison)," were Mandela's words to his fellow black Africans.

The Botha government could not agree to Mandela's terms, so Mandela and the Rivonia group stayed in jail.

From 1985 forward, Mandela's release would be demanded by many countries around the world, including the United States, where daily demonstrations took place outside the South African embassy in Washington, D.C. Black Americans in Congress formed the Trans-Africa Organization started by Congressman Randall Robinson for the purpose of supporting black Africans in their struggle against apartheid.

Finally, in 1987, President Reagan, under public pressure, placed sanctions against South Africa. This measure prevented American businesses from investing there and encouraged the withdrawal of existing investments. University students, particularly, insisted that university endowment funds be withdrawn, or divested, from South African investments. This was an effective way to express their disapproval of apartheid. The hope was that if its economy lost enough money, South Africa would give up apartheid in order to open the doors to foreign investors.

Even though the ANC leaders were still in jail and refusing to cooperate, Botha started making further changes in the apartheid system. In 1985 the pass laws were abolished, and in 1986 blacks were granted freedom of movement in urban areas. Hotels and restaurants were opened to all races, along with some theaters; nonwhites were allowed to emigrate out of South Africa. In 1987 some beaches abolished racial

restrictions, and jobs—once secure for whites only—
were open to all. By 1988 commuter trains were
desegregated. By 1989 certain residential areas in Johannesburg were opened to all races.

In the midst of these turbulent times, Winnie
Mandela's words and actions reached the headlines.
Some blacks were hired by the police to spy on the
ANC. A black traitor to his people could be subject
to the practice of "necklacing." In this cruel form of
torture, a rubber tire is soaked in gasoline, hung
around the neck of the traitor, and set afire. One shoe
is left to identify the burned body.

In 1986 Winnie Mandela made this statement
about the event. "With our matchboxes and neck-
laces, we will liberate this country." Her comments in-
furiated the whites and sent Mrs. Mandela tumbling
from her pedestal.

Two years later, another incident further
damaged her image. After Winnie returned from
Brandfort and took up residence in her new home in
Soweto, she tried to help troubled teenage boys by taking them into her home. They became her bodyguards
and were called the "Mandela United Football Club."
As a woman living alone, she earned the disapproval
of some members of the ANC. She seemed to be more
radical than her husband.

When a 14-year-old boy, Stoempie Moeketsi Seipi, was stabbed to death by one or more of her young bodyguards, rumors blamed Winnie Mandela for the murder.

In 1989 Nelson Mandela was moved from Pollsmoor to Victor Verster Prison. While Winnie was in the headlines, Nelson found himself in a modern bungalow with three bedrooms and a swimming pool—a different environment from the bare cells of 26 years. Despite this comfort, Nelson Mandela was not only lonely but worried about his wife.

In 1989, while Mandela was fretting in Victor Verster, President P. W. Botha suffered a stroke and Frederick W. de Klerk was elected and assumed office. De Klerk was a lawyer, known as a man of moderation and integrity. Economic sanctions were hurting the economy, and world opinion had turned dramatically against South Africa. Realizing it was time for change, de Klerk was quietly negotiating with Nelson Mandela behind the scenes. Mandela compromised on a gradual schedule for dismantling apartheid.

When Mandela's release and the legalization of the ANC were announced, the world was amazed. Mandela himself was told of the release only the night before. Reporters and television crews flew to Cape Town and set up their equipment outside Victor Verster Prison early on February 11, 1990.

The great day—February 11, 1990. Nelson and Winnie Mandela acknowledge the crowds in Cape Town.

The wait seemed forever. The time of Mandela's release was delayed by three hours because the key members of the ANC had to come from different parts of South Africa. When they were all assembled, Nelson, with Winnie beside him, walked through the gates to freedom.

A grand reception awaited Mandela at the stadium in the township of Soweto and at his old home outside Johannesburg. He met the press and friends at his small house before moving into the spacious residence that his wife had built behind high brick walls. The money for building this house came from the royalties Mandela had received from his book, *The Struggle Is My Life*, published in 1986.

As Nelson became involved in talks with President de Klerk, the scandal about Winnie resurfaced. Her three months' trial cast a shadow over Mandela's leadership of the ANC.

In South African law, a jury does not determine the guilt or innocence of a person—a judge does. On May 13 and 14 of 1991, Judge Michael Stegman found Winnie Mandela guilty of involvement in this case. She was sentenced to six years in prison: five years for kidnapping and one year as an accessory to the fact. Her lawyers appealed and hoped to have the charges dismissed. If the appeal failed, some observers believed that President de Klerk might issue her a full pardon. Whatever the outcome of the trial, Mr. Mandela vowed to support and stand by his wife, just as she had stood by him all the years he was in prison.

As Mandela struggled with political problems among blacks and negotiations with the government, people asked what the future of South Africa would be? Would there be renaissance or revolution ahead?

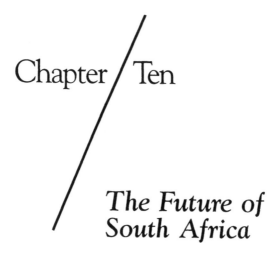

Chapter / Ten

The Future of South Africa

At the toe of South Africa, the warm waters of the Indian Ocean clash with the cold currents of the Atlantic Ocean. Swirling, deadly tides have threatened ships for centuries. Many vessels have bucked and plowed perilously through these choppy seas until they reached Cape Town's safe harbor.

The place of confrontation between these two oceans is called the Cape of Good Hope. Nowadays, symbolically, the clashes are not only between oceans but between blacks.

The tide of black violence comes from the two largest tribes, the Xhosas and the Zulus. Tribal enemies for centuries, they are political rivals, too—the Xhosas of the ANC feuding with the Zulus of the IFP (Inkatha Freedom Party). There are some exceptions.

Chief Mangosuthu Buthelezi, leader of the Inkatha Party

A small number of Zulus belong to the ANC, but very few Xhosas have membership in the IFP.

Since the ANC dates back to 1912, it has a longer and older tradition. The Inkatha Freedom Party, however, began in 1975 as a cultural organization and gradually shifted to a political movement headed by Chief Mangosuthu Buthelezi. Appointed chief executive officer of the KwaZulu territory (once called Zululand) in 1970, Buthelezi governs nearly seven million Zulus. Almost two million of them are active members of the IFP.

When the South African government created ten separate homelands for blacks, Buthelezi successfully resisted making KwaZulu into a homeland. Blacks—other than Zulus—respected him for this.

But Buthelezi's philosophy on other issues made him unpopular with non-Zulus. Unlike Mandela, Buthelezi was against economic sanctions. He felt that they deprived black Africans of jobs. Buthelezi was also against violence and armed struggle as a means of toppling apartheid. Buthelezi's attitude on sanctions and violence was similar to that of the white government. This made him suspicious to the ANC and other blacks.

By contrast, in 1962 Mandela had abandoned nonviolence in favor of armed struggle. After he assumed power as head of the ANC in 1990, he insisted that the international community keep sanctions in place until every condition for overturning apartheid was met.

Yet another major difference between the two black leaders of the two major parties was their attitude toward communism. Buthelezi strongly opposed communism while Mandela supported the South African Communist Party and accepted communists into the ANC membership. Mandela suggested that nationalizing some industries was necessary, whereas Buthelezi advocated a free enterprise system for South

Africa. But they agreed on a democracy and Bill of Rights for South Africa.

Mandela and Buthelezi actually had close personal ties. Although considerably younger than Mandela, Buthelezi had also attended the University of Fort Hare. During the many years Mandela was in prison, Buthelezi tried to get him released. He had even refused to begin talks with President P. W. Botha in 1985 unless Nelson Mandela was included.

Because of the Xhosa and Zulu rivalry, and because of their political differences, Mandela and Buthelezi became opponents. Once Mandela was free, both men wanted to meet publicly. However, Mandela's ANC advisers held him back. They claimed the time was not right. Almost a year would pass before the two men met officially. In the interim, violence among blacks was worsening. From 1986 to 1991, 6,000 Xhosas and Zulus killed each other in Natal, Soweto, and other townships around Johannesburg.

Other factors contributed to the black-against-black violence. The economic sanctions against South Africa resulted in high unemployment. Young men without jobs and educations were using their idle time to fight one another.

If Mandela and Buthelezi had problems, so did President de Klerk. Although a champion for racial justice in the eyes of the world, he had become a lone-

The key to the future: Mandela and President de Klerk shake hands at their first meeting.

ly and embattled man among his own Afrikaner people. Many of them wanted to keep apartheid to preserve their Afrikaner culture. However, most of the whites from the British section of the population supported de Klerk's new policies.

De Klerk released Mandela and lifted the ban on the ANC in February 1990, but talks between de Klerk and Mandela were the key to removing *all* phases of apartheid. These official meetings began on May 2, 1990. The first session was called the Groote Schuur Minute. Groote Schuur, once the home of Cecil John Rhodes in Cape Town, was the official residence for the three-day meeting. One condition agreed upon was the release of political prisoners from Robben Island.

The next meeting on August 6, 1990, was called the Pretoria Minute. During this 15-hour formal session in Pretoria, the two men worked out the legal mechanics for moving the ANC and the government forward in their efforts to dismantle apartheid. After that meeting, Mandela suspended the "armed struggle," but insisted that economic sanctions remain. Aside from these formal meetings, Mandela and de Klerk often had weekly or daily communications, particularly when the black violence in the townships erupted. They appeared to have a warm and trusting relationship.

Meanwhile, Buthelezi was apparently ignored by the government and Mandela. Obviously, he wanted a voice in the negotiations. "With a paid up membership of nearly two million South Africans of all races, the IFP sees itself, justifiably, as being a major player at the negotiation table. I have repeatedly warned against bi-polar negotiations between the South African government and the ANC, in which the other parties would line up behind one or the other," said Buthelezi to this author.

Apartheid, however, was already doomed. When Parliament opened in Cape Town in February 1991, de Klerk's introductory statement startled members of

the white Conservative Party (CP). Many stalked angrily out of the chamber to protest.

"There is no room for injustice, tyranny, domination, violence, or social degradation and economic
decline. The elimination of racial discrimination goes
hand in hand with the constitutional process," said
President de Klerk. The remaining pillars of apartheid—the Group Areas Act, the Population Registration Act, and the Land Acts of 1913 and 1936 were
removed in June of 1991. The results brought some
whites into bloody conflict with blacks. When black
squatters rebuilt shacks of corrugated iron and wood
on the property of white farmers, the police fought off
angry whites. These questions of land rights may take
time to solve.

The reaction to de Klerk's remarks ranged from
applause to outrage. The Conservative Party wanted
to maintain white purity. But to the right of the CP
was the AWB, a radical resistance group of white
Afrikaners led by Eugene TerreBlanche. He and his
followers carried guns and were ready to fight blacks
to maintain white supremacy. To protest de Klerk's
announcement, the Afrikaner farmers drove their
tractors into the center of Pretoria.

The more militant members of the ANC also
reacted against de Klerk's proposals. They shouted
and sang of their displeasure in the streets of Cape

Town. De Klerk's master plan to crush apartheid was not fast enough or strong enough for them.

Unfortunately, Mandela couldn't deliver the rights of freedom quickly enough to satisfy the radical black youth. He was not able to stop the violence nor was he able to increase the membership of the ANC beyond 150,000 during his first year as a free man.

Another liability to Mandela's leadership was his continued support for dictator Fidel Castro of Cuba; Muammar Qaddafi of Libya; and Yasir Arafat of the Palestinian Liberation Organization. This allegiance shocked the western world. Nelson Mandela, a man intensely loyal to those who supported the ANC cause in the 1960s, would not forsake these allies to play the game of politics.

However, in July of 1991, Mandela's followers demonstrated their confidence in him. For the first time in 30 years, the ANC was free to hold its conference. With over 2,000 delegates represented in Durban, Nelson Mandela was elected president, replacing Oliver Tambo, who became national chairman.

Also in July, the political scandal (called "Inkathagate") was uncovered. The government admitted giving secret funds—amounting to $500,000—to the IFP, allegedly for political rallies in 1989 and 1990. This financial backing was interpreted as a gift to Inkatha for opposing sanctions. Violence and betrayal of the ANC were the results. For over a year, Mandela had accused the government of promoting violence in the townships.

De Klerk demoted the two ministers involved, and talks with Mandela continued. In fact, a Peace Accord to end the violence was signed among de Klerk, Mandela, and Buthelezi in the summer of 1991. However, a multi-party conference at the end of 1991 set the tone for negotiations on the 700-page report from a legal commission for a new constitution, containing a bill of rights. By 1994, a democratic election is expected to be held.

At long last the apartheid laws have been repealed, but South Africa is still beset by huge problems facing its population of 40 million, of whom 30 million are black. Lack of housing, unemployment, inadequate education, and crime are some of the major ones. When apartheid restrictions were lifted, a flood of blacks left the homelands to come to the cities, looking for work. Seven million people built houses of cardboard and corrugated iron outside the cities. The population of young black men under the age of 27 was 70 percent and unemployment soared to 53 percent. With the lifting of sanctions, the government hopes new factories and more jobs will reduce unemployment.

Then, too, the educational system for black children must be reorganized to reach the same standards as that for white youngsters. The cost will be high. Whether whites can carry these costs and train qualified black teachers right away remains to be seen.

Despite these enormous problems, positive signs have emerged. Blacks have started their own business-es (*spazas*) in townships and homelands. Minivan taxis have become a multimillion-dollar business. Small vendors are free to spread their wares on the streets of Johannesburg and Durban to sell to tourists. Stands in front yards, repair shops in backyards, and fast-food restaurants have sprung up in the townships.

Writing a new constitution, establishing equal voting rights, and holding a free election in 1994 are pressing needs. If the violence can be contained, for-eign investment could possibly relieve some of the problems. But none of them can be solved overnight.

Whatever takes place in the next few years, Nel-son Mandela's place in history is assured. The fact that he served 27 years in prison for his belief in freedom and equality for nonwhites has brought him honors and worldwide recognition. His aura of dignity, his countenance of kindness, and his irrepressible sense of humor impress all who meet him.

Perhaps the title of Mandela's book, *No Easy Walk to Freedom*, best describes the end of apartheid and the birth of a free South Africa.

Selected Bibliography

Books

Benson, Mary. *Nelson Mandela: The Man and the Movement.* New York: W. W. Norton & Co., 1986.

Berger, Peter L., and Bobby Godsell. *A Future South Africa.* Cape Town, South Africa: Human & Rousseau, and Tafelberg, 1988.

Harrison, Nancy. *Winnie Mandela.* New York: George Braziller, 1986.

Haskins, Jim. *Winnie Mandela: A Life of Struggle.* New York: G. P. Putnam's Sons, 1988.

Lelyveld, Joseph. *Move Your Shadow South Africa, Black and White.* New York: Times Books, 1985.

Mandela, Nelson. *No Easy Walk to Freedom.* London: Heinemann, 1965.

——. *The Struggle Is My Life.* New York: Pathfinder Press, 1986.

Mandela, Winnie. *Part of My Soul Went with Him.* New York: W. W. Norton & Co., 1984.

Meer, Fatima. *Higher Than Hope.* New York: Harper & Row, 1988.

Tutu, Desmond. *Hope and Suffering.* Grand Rapids, Michigan: William B. Eerdmans Publishing Co., 1984.

Villet, Barbara. *Blood River.* New York: Everest House, 1982.

Magazines

Economist. February 17, 1990. "The Right Wing Flaps," "The Buthelezi Factor," and "Sanction-monious."

Essence Magazine. July 1989. "Word from South Africa."

Fort Harian. The University of Fort Hare in the Republic of Ciskei. September/December 1989. "The Inauguration of the De Beers Centenary Art Gallery."

Leadership Magazine. Cape Town, South Africa. "The Dawn of Reason." Peter Younghusband.

Maclean's. February 10, 1990. "A Bold Move." Holger Jensen and Chris Erasmus.

Maclean's. February 12, 1990. "Tearing Down the System." John Bierman, Chris Erasmus, William Lowther, Ross Laver.

Maclean's. February 27, 1990. "Scandal in Soweto." John Bierman.

Monitor Magazine. Port Elizabeth, South Africa. April 1990. "No Easy Walk To Freedom." Rory Riordan.

The Nation. March 12, 1990. "Negotiating a Nonracial Democracy." Fatima Meer.

National Review. March 5, 1990. "Solidarity with ANC?" Radek Sikorski.

The New Republic. March 13, 1990. "Winnie the Shrew." Steven Mufson.

People Magazine. February 18, 1990. "Maki Mandela." William Plummer and S. Avery Brown.

People Magazine. April 9, 1990. "Hope Meets Hatred in South Africa." Michael Ryan.

Scholastic Update. February 12, 1990. "Voices for Their People's Pain." David Oliver Relin.

U.S. News & World Report. August 20, 1990. "The Mandela Quandary." Robin Knight and Jim Jones.

U.S. News & World Report. October 8, 1990. "South Africa: Cry the Beloved Country." Steven Roberts.

Newspapers

Business Day. (Johannesburg, South Africa) August 9–29, 1990.

The Christian Science Monitor. February through November 1990. Articles by John Battersby.

St. Petersburg Times. June 10, 1990. "CIA Tip Reportedly Led to Mandela Arrest, Decades in Jail." Joseph Albright and Marcia Kunstel of Cox News Service.

The Weekly Mail. (Johannesburg, South Africa) August 9–29, 1990.

Index

ADDENDUM

Since this book was first published, Nelson
Mandela has become a world statesman. In 1993
Mandela and then-President F. W. de Klerk received
the Nobel Peace Prize for their efforts to end
apartheid and build a democratic South Africa.
Together, as lawyers, the two men wrote a new
constitution.

By May 1994 and at the age of 75, Mandela was
the first African to be elected President of South
Africa. Winnie and Nelson divorced in 1994.

Great Britain's Queen Elizabeth visited the new
President of South Africa in March of 1995.

On his 80th birthday in 1998 Nelson Mandela
found love once again. He married Graca Machel,
the widow of a Mozambican president and black
liberation leader. His new wife was described as
"Africa's Jacqueline Kennedy." Shortly thereafter
Mandela was awarded an honorary doctor of law
degree at Harvard University for bringing racial
justice to his country. More than 50 honorary
degrees have been awarded to Mandela.

Mandela's presidency came to an end on March
27, 1999, when he resigned to allow Thabo Mbeki
to become his successor.

Against tremendous odds, Nelson Mandela will
go down in history as a man of outstanding character
and accomplishments.

Made in the USA
San Bernardino, CA
07 May 2015